the Dai . story
Morris
SHADOW

the **Dai**. story

Morris
SHADOW

DAI MORRIS

WITH

MARTYN WILLIAMS

This book is dedicated to
Marlene, Helen, Greg, Ben, Abigail and Joseph

First impression: 2012
Second impression: 2012

© Copyright Dai Morris and Y Lolfa Cyf., 2012

The contents of this book are subject to copyright, and may
not be reproduced by any means, mechanical or electronic,
without the prior, written consent of the publishers.

The publishers wish to acknowledge the support of
Cyngor Llyfrau Cymru

Cover design: Y Lolfa

Every attempt was made to ascertain
and contact the source of all the photographs in this book

ISBN: 978 184771 486 2

FSC
Published and printed in Wales
on paper from well maintained forests by
Y Lolfa Cyf., Talybont, Ceredigion SY24 5HE
website www.ylolfa.com
e-mail ylolfa@ylolfa.com
tel 01970 832 304
fax 832 782

34

CAPS FOR WALES

3

FIVE NATIONS CHAMPIONSHIPS

2

TRIPLE CROWNS

1

GRAND SLAM

414

GAMES FOR NEATH

Diolch
Thank you

My thanks to all the contributors – I am humbled by some of the comments made by family, friends and so many players. Sadly, two of my great friends and contributors to this book, Brian Thomas and Peter Davies, are no longer with us. They were Neath stalwarts, and I have included their memories and stories alongside those of their mates and fellow players. The great Mervyn Davies has also left us. It has not been a good year.

Thank you Max for your kind words, not only now, but over the years.

I am grateful as well to those who have loaned photographs and memorabilia – my memory is not what it used to be, and I did need reminding of quite a few things. So, thanks to Paul Hart, David Price, Glen Ball, Dai Parker, Rugby Relics, Vince Good and the Rhigos boys.

Y Lolfa must be a brave publishing house to commit themselves to a book about a 70-year-old former rugby player. My thanks, also, to the Welsh Books Council for its support.

Naturally, I am indebted to the writer and broadcaster Martyn Williams, for suggesting the idea of this book and his dedication, tolerance and enthusiasm in completing my story. He's had easier tasks.

If I said to Martyn "I can't remember" once, I must have said that a few thousand times, and if there are errors, they are mine – because it was such a long time ago.

Contents

Foreword
by Max Boyce

Dai – The Shadow

I CONSIDER IT a great honour to be asked to write a short foreword to this book, so aptly named *The Shadow* – an overdue tribute to Dai Morris. In rugby terms, he is the definitive working-class hero.

> Now Dai works down at Tower
> The pit called No. 4
> Some say that he was quarried
> From rock, a mile below
> He goes to work each morning
> Much the same as you or I
> The foreman calls him, "Mister"
> But the children call him Dai.

I'm sure that everyone who was asked to contribute to this book agreed only too readily in an attempt to say thank you and pay a deserved tribute to a very special person. One of the greatest players to wear the Welsh jersey.

A Rhigos boy, born and bred, who, in his early rugby career, went also to play with great distinction for my village side Glynneath, and was part of that great 'invincible' side at Abernant Park in 1962.

He then moved 'a short pair of rails' down the valley to

Neath where he was 'forged' – the furnace at the Gnoll where the incessant chants of "Neath, Neath, Neath" struck fear into the hearts of the strongest of men.

But it was with Wales, in the halcyon days of the 1970s, that this true legend was born.

In those crowning years Wales were blessed with so many brilliant players, with seemingly God-given gifts. But those mercurial players needed 'footings' – a foundation; a setting in which their diamonds could shine the brightest.

David Morris was one of those often unsung heroes who were part of the integral foundation of Wales's rugby success in those memorable times.

I have always thought it was a great shame that he was never selected for the British Lions.

> Some say that Dai was much too small
> This man who works with Iron
> And that's the reason why they say
> He was never made a Lion
> And though they never picked him
> "'Na fe bois. Fel na mae", [That's how it goes]
> There's none that's played
> Though light he weighed
> More 'genuine' than Dai.

When David Morris played for the combined Neath and Aberavon side that lost 43–4 to New Zealand in 1973, I wrote:

> They didn't keep the score up long
> And we chipped in for a wreath
> Neath blamed Aberavon
> And Aberavon blamed Neath
> Some there blamed the linesman
> Some blamed you and I
> We all blamed the Committee
> But no-one there blamed Dai.

When he was forced to retire from international rugby with a knee injury, it was typical of Dai that he finished his playing career with his village team Rhigos, and playing with the sons of the fathers he grew up with on the 'oxygenic' slopes of the Rhigos Mountain.

Perhaps, there have been more celebrated players in the history of Welsh rugby, but none that is more respected than this gentleman of rugby who's affectionately known to all as Dai.

A shy, unassuming person, who gave his all, at all times and asked for nothing in return. He is one of the most genuine people I have ever met, which is why I admire him more than any of the other players I know.

The respect in which he is held, by so many people and players, is testimony to his character and the honest way he played the game.

That respect is something that has to be earned. It is not given easily, or freely – and is afforded to only the few.

Max Boyce
October 2012

1

Dai Morris

I PLEADED WITH the nurses at Neath General Hospital not to contact Marlene my wife. They had already told me that I had cracked a few ribs, but the pain would be nothing compared to Marlene's tongue lashing.

You have no idea.

She had hidden my rugby boots in the garage, never to be exhumed again. I had ambitions of continuing to play for Rhigos, in the same team as my son Greg. But she tried to put a stop to the 'romantic nonsense'.

"You are not playing bloody rugby again," was the eleventh commandment, and the boots went. But not far!

So, when the phone call came early on a Saturday afternoon from the boys to tell me that my home village team of Rhigos was short of players and subs for a league game against Neath Athletic at Cwrt Herbert Fields, I didn't hesitate. I also knew that Greg was playing as well. I found the boots, because I knew where they were. Marlene saw me – and threw a real 'wobbly'.

"If you go down there with those boots, you'll get a bump – I am telling you now!" There were a few more threats as well, but I won't dwell on those. I swear she bewitched me that day, but along I went to help out. It was one ruck too many, and I got caught, with my ribcage exposed, by an ex-Resolven prop, whose name I cannot remember. No doubt he is still drinking on his fame.

Later, I was told that Marlene was contacted by some Rhigos neighbours, telling her that her Dai was in Neath General Hospital. I still have suspicions that the informer was one of my best mates and fellow Neath player Dai Parker. I know Greg wouldn't have spilt the beans. So it must have been him, the little one, because he was at the game!

Whoever it was, Marlene was on her way, and there would be no escape. I'd rather be trampled by a pack of raging All Blacks than face the prospect of what punishment was to come. I was not disappointed!

It was to be my last league game. I was fifty-two years old.

But it wasn't quite my last game of rugby...

2

Rhigos

Introduction by Ken Grindle

I HAVE KNOWN Dai all my life. He was a little older than me, but we both went to the same primary school in Rhigos. The Morris family, Ben and Ivy May, were extremely kind to us as a family, because they were doing very well with thirsty colliers at the New Inn and were exceptionally generous – too generous in fact. Rhigos at that time was only a third of the size it is now, but there were more children there – and we would all innocently wander in and out of each other's houses at will. The Morris family also had livestock, sheep, milking cows and a few ponies over the years. That was a big local attraction to us kids. The Morris family loved kids and animals.

Dai still has stray cats around his house, a dog inside, and his horses of course, but I can remember his first four-legged adoptee. Dai was about thirteen then, I think. It was a sad, ragged-looking sheep, wandering around Rhigos looking for food. Sheep (intelligent Welsh sheep, that is) could unlock gates in those days, and ruin a garden. Dai though, started feeding this one discarded sheep with bottled milk, and the animal, by now named Mary, started following Dai around the village, wherever he went.

Dai with Mary behind him was a sight to behold.

The same happened when he found an abandoned boxer – who stayed with him for years.

And if you travelled with him in a car, and he thought a bird had been hit, that was it. Pandemonium! You had to stop and pick the bird up, and take it home. One of the 'hardest' men to play rugby in Wales – my foot!

At the risk of Dai having one of his famous 'pouts', which I know from first-hand experience could last a few weeks, I will say that when he went to join Glynneath Youth he was clueless as a rugby player. But what an athlete! He could run all day, and gradually through work, he built up the amazing strength that was to make him possibly the strongest thirteen-stone forward ever. He and the likes of his colliery mates Glyn Shaw and Graham Donovan could haul, lift or push anything. Dai's legs, I swear, were made of granite, he had hands of steel and his endurance is legendary. I know for a fact that he played six games in one week, a WRU Cup final, two sevens tournaments, turned up for two invitational sides and off he went somewhere else as well. Unbelievable, since he was also working throughout the week. He could not say "no" to a game of rugby.

He joined Glynneath Youth as a centre or wing, but the making of Dai was the company of people like John and Dai Weaver and Lyn Tregonning in the Glynneath 1st XV. They had their undefeated 'invincible' season, a remarkable feat, and then had to beat Pontypool United – also undefeated – in the penultimate game of the season. Dai must have been immense in that game, since one of the boys, Gareth Owens, came back and proclaimed "Dai Morris has arrived!" He left Glynneath having scored twenty-two tries in a season as a number 8.

Ken Grindle
Neighbour, and school friend

* * *

My life has been moulded by the three 'Rs' – Rhigos, rugby and racing horses, and it has been a life of joy. I mean that.

I have met famous people, politicians and pop stars, great players and fantastic opponents, but at the top of my list are the people I grew up with.

My favourite road has always been the homeward journey to Rhigos – a place where I am comfortable in the company of family, friends and its challenging terrain. I have visited several marvellous places, but have not known them. Rhigos is where I was born, where I have lived nearly all my life – and will probably be buried there as well. I did spend some time living with Marlene and her mother in a flat in Glynneath – about five miles away!

When abroad on a foreign rugby tour someone would ask what the time was. An answer was given, but then I would tell them the time in Rhigos, since I would never alter my watch from the Rhigos time zone.

Yet, we were not people driven by clocks and timetables, and very often, I suspect, time has stood still, on the mountain and moor.

For those who have not visited Rhigos, it is above Aberdare, beyond Hirwaun, to the left of Merthyr, and below Brecon. Can't be clearer than that, can I? Most people drive through and don't stop.

You could say it is now a forgotten place. The Germans only bombed it once, and I suspect that the pilot was only offloading his cargo for the flight home. But it was, I am told, a matter of great concern that Rhigos had been targeted by the Luftwaffe!

But for two centuries the people of Rhigos had survived famine, cholera, hunger and poverty. It has experienced huge boom and bust economic periods. The area has faced immense challenges, and some would argue that we are still to this day the forgotten place. That is until an unpopular development needs to be sited there like gas tanks, waste disposal plants or wind turbines. Then, suddenly, Hirwaun and Rhigos top the governmental location lists.

Little wonder why we have become a defiant lot. It is our nature.

We created coal mines with most of my family involved in dangerous sinking developments underground. Health and safety was something for the future in those dark days. A twelve-month sit-in campaign halted the Gas Tank Scheme in the 1970s and it was the Hirwaun and Rhigos miners who fought and bought Tower Colliery to keep it open. That, too, is now sadly closed, a place where I worked, but I am proud of our defiance. It is in the blood.

The Welsh Government has a Communities First programme, full of initiatives. They should have come to Rhigos for advice. We've suffered more initiatives than anyone.

First, the Hirwaun ironworks dominated everything, followed by coal, which in turn brought the railway and Brunel. People came from far and wide to Hirwaun and Rhigos in those days. The Irish arrived in droves escaping famine in their homeland, attracted by the prospect of work. So, too, did the Italians and the Polish. People moved from west Wales as well. Chapels, schools and pubs were built, but the housing was poor and temporary. The new people had to be resourceful, and a plot of borrowed or available land next to the worker's shanty villages provided root crops and grazing for goats, pigs and cattle. Pay was paltry, as the ironworks and colliery owners became richer.

The Hirwaun 'iron age' came to an end as the steam coal mines of the Rhondda offered better prospects. So the people moved away, and those left behind waited for another recovery or discovery. The feast or famine periods have left their scars, especially on the landscape and its people.

Our family was not immune to these economic challenges. My father, Benjamin, was the eldest of four children, who were looked after by their grandmother, since his mother had died very young. His father, however, remarried, and somehow between colliery shifts, they also ran a grocery credit store in Seven Sisters. It had to close because people could not pay their bills during the colliers' strike.

For most, including my family, life was the coal-pit life – roof falls, methane gas escapes, despair, accidents, death and tragedy. Work for the pit boys began at 6.30 a.m. in two-foot seams and they surfaced at 3.30 p.m. They worked for six days and were paid 13s 8d per week. Yet, I recall my uncle telling me that though they had no bath, radio, television or modern gadgets, neither did they have locked doors or have robberies – because there was nothing to steal.

My father, Ben, kept animals: a pig at the bottom of the garden, chickens in the yard and he also kept pigeons. But he left for Somerset in 1926 during the General Strike and returned to Rhigos with his wife Ivy May in 1940.

He worked as a blacksmith at the Onllwyn Colliery, and they both ran the New Inn pub in Rhigos. My father met his customers at the pit in the morning, and then served them pints in the evening.

Ironically, it was the Second World War that brought some prosperity to the area. Until then, people had made a living on the land, or underneath it in the numerous small collieries dotted around the Rhondda and Cynon Valley. Younger folk didn't fancy working underground, unless they had to, and others moved away or enlisted in the forces. This had a profound effect on Rhigos as a community, which was largely Welsh-speaking.

But, during the war, the German bombers had found the

munitions factories of south-east England easy targets, and so the war department reacted and decided to build a munitions factory at Rhigos. It was deemed remote enough.

Even now, the Welsh Government has failed to find and help Rhigos, so how on earth would the German bombers find it? But in those days it was work for the locals, which meant weekly payslips. It also brought life to the village, and I assume that even the German bombers would have had difficulty in finding Rhigos and the munitions factory through the mountain mist.

It attracted new people into the area who needed housing, or at least a roof over their heads. Once again, these were hastily put up timber-framed or prefab houses, hardly robust enough to withstand the mountain-top weather of Rhigos. There is better housing there now, but some of the earlier houses still remain.

I live in one.

Naturally, I was oblivious to all of this, having been born in 1941 in the New Inn, Rhigos – my parents' pub.

I wasn't oblivious to when the war had ended. I knew because people talked and, as kids, we heard that the ROF – the munitions factory – was to be closed, leaving hundreds of people out of work again, and most moved on, leaving the hastily built homes empty and the war factory a relic. More importantly, it would take customers away from the New Inn!

But the country had to rebuild after the war, create a new economy, and the government established an industrial site on our doorstep, with 'grand' street names like Fifth Avenue, Fourth Avenue and so on.

Fifth Avenue in Hirwaun and Rhigos! Weh-he! They are still there – the street names, that is.

Better housing came too. So did large companies such as GEC, Hitachi, Morgan and Brace, Dunloppillo and Sobell.

Work was assured, but even they didn't last long, and have long disappeared. Another boom and bust period for our community! Fifth Avenue is now deserted. But, for a while, these were good times, and my home, the pub, prospered.

My father was originally from Banwen, a village over the mountain in the Swansea valley. He was a Welsh speaker, as were most of the Rhigos folk. When he returned from Midsomer Norton in Somerset, my sisters, Roselle and Ann, had already been born. Colin, my younger brother, and I were born in the New Inn pub in Rhigos.

My mother was one of the hardest working women ever. She cooked, served and took care of four children: my sisters, Colin and me.

How that was accomplished I will never know; it was sheer hard work but she was always there for us, and made sure, as youngsters, that we were all in bed by six – before opening time. She never touched a drop of drink. The pub was closed on Sundays, but we were still in bed by six, because that was whist night for my parents and a few 'special' locals.

Living in a pub did have its challenges, and at the age of two, I was run over by a beer lorry, and though I wouldn't say I was accident prone, I also have the scar on my hand today from lunging for tadpoles and finding broken glass at the bottom of a local pool.

The highlight for us as kids was the annual show held at the back of the pub, and in winter, to see the Banwen Miners' Hunt gather outside. There were point-to-point races nearby as well, and it wasn't long before I became the owner of Twts, a pony who managed to break my kneecap with a well-aimed kick. The memory of it still hurts.

On our rented field, behind the pub, we had chickens and dogs; if we had found a giraffe roaming around we would have kept it.

I also had a milking cow, and this might also explain

my passion for milk. I have drunk little alcohol, but milk I used to drink eight pints a day when working down under and playing on weekends. I still drink a fair amount. But, ironically, I hated being a milk monitor in the local primary school. I didn't learn much there, but I do remember spending hours looking out through the window – at the exciting world outside.

As we grew a little older, we were allowed out to explore and play – and what a theme park it was, and it was ours.

We had hills, moors and mountains to roam, pools to swim in, farmers looking for some help with haymaking. We would stay out until dusk playing football, or any sport that was competitive. Two coats placed on a field were enough for a game.

We knew just about everybody, since most would come in and out of our front door. The pub was always active, and Mam's cooking of pastries was legendary. Tripe and onions was another speciality. There was, at the beginning, a men's only bar, and not even my mother was allowed in there. So I would listen, when allowed, to the tales of miners, farmers, Irish travellers and anybody else who passed through. Not many of the locals would pass by, except for the chapel goers.

My mother, father and our helper Wally Hoffland kept a good house. If you had seen the size of both men, you would understand that we rarely had trouble.

Few of the locals were known by surnames. They, and their animals, were known by their farms – Tŷ Draw, Tai Cwpla, Cwm Hwnt, Hendre Fawr, Torch y Garredd, Tŷ Dewi, Penwau, Beili Glas – or more graphically by their trade or work at the Pandy Colliery. There was Dai 'Pumps' and Fred 'Rats' – and there's no need to explain what they did down under. Their horses were named after them as well!

Rhigos was also where I nurtured my love for animals

and wildlife. I think I inherited it from my father as well, who could not be spoken to when reading the weekly *Pigeon Fancier*.

My friends keep reminding me of when I found an injured magpie. I looked after it and fed it until it became so tame that it would perch itself on my shoulder as we walked the hills, the streets and to school! It waited for me to come out through the front door of the New Inn every morning for about four years. So there I was, with a bird on my shoulder, feathered in Neath colours!

I don't know why I have this fondness for animals but I would have made a lousy farmer. I couldn't stand the thought of breeding sheep, pigs or cattle and then killing them. Much later in life, I was able to rent some 50 acres where I kept two Hereford Cross cattle and some 120 sheep. "Hopeless farmer but a good feeder", as Ken Grindle says, who also remembers me adopting a stray sheep called Mary, which followed me around the village. The thought of breeding animals to be slaughtered did not appeal at all. Some say I am the same today, because I have often been told to be a bit more ruthless with the horses. It's just not in my nature.

Marlene, my wife, always says, "If I come back in another life, I would like to come back as a four-legged furry animal – and to be looked after by Dai Morris!"

I suppose I was destined to follow my father to the mines. The village of Rhigos also had its own mine, the Pandy, and life, habits and activities were determined by the mine's shifts.

Though it isn't possible, if I had the opportunity, I would gladly return to the mines – even now. It is the comradeship that I miss, the banter and the leg pulling – the simplicity of it all. The boys underground at Pandy and Hirwaun collieries saw more of each other than they did of their families, and there were no airs and graces about them. They were an additional family. There were short men with tall tales, tall men with taller tales. But, they were all 'butties'.

We shared grievances, problems and anything that threatened our community. I have to admit, the chat was mostly about rugby, bets and tests of strength and speed. Those who were not competitive would bet, those who were, would brag.

These were the inhabitants of Rhigos, perched or nested on the mountainside of the Cynon Valley. It is probably better known now or familiar to radio listeners as the first road to close when there is wintry weather around. It is that remote, but for me, it is, and has always been rather special.

It was here that I grew from being an asthmatic child, sometimes being unable to walk more than a few yards, to a young man, being tested on a daily basis in moving and lifting heavy machinery. And it was competitive too. Talk to any miner, especially those of pre-Thatcher days, and the underground 'chat' would always have been of endurance, strength and survival. It was always the talk of men – and then of the village, and of course the New Inn.

But, before earning my keep, I had to start my education, and that meant the local primary school and then the Gadlys Secondary Modern in Aberdare. The biggest wrench of all was having to leave the pub, become sort of organised and face what was to become the biggest bore of all – education. But don't let my grandchildren read this!

3

School

I COULD HARDLY be called academic. By that, I mean reading books, literature or studying physics and chemistry – and, above all, understanding them.

Yet, by the time I reached high school or secondary modern age, I knew a great deal about life and survival. But there is no hiding the fact that I was pretty dull as far as exam results were concerned.

There was initially the challenge of the local primary school in Rhigos. I simply did not want to attend. They made me a milk monitor – a job that I hated. I couldn't wait for the last bell of the afternoon and to run back home. From the day I started, I wanted to leave. I don't remember if anything complimentary was ever written about me in any school report. Capable milk monitor perhaps?

You are no 'innocent' as a youngster living in a mining community pub. Life in a village and colliery pub is an everlasting marvellous exposure to men's chat and their worries, grievances and characters. These men and their wives were kind and compassionate, heroes and heroines. With their unwashed coal mascara eyes, these men were my father's friends, and each one to me as a young child was a friend of mine, but, they were also frail.

My mother, more than my father, could have filled the scripts of *Coronation Street* for years with tales that were told, some true, some tragic, but there was always laughter.

Colliery men live in darkness more than light. I've never met people like them in Cardiff and far-flung places. They were honest, dishonest, boisterous and quiet. But they were men who lived on the edge. There are no secrets underground. If you did harbour one – it would soon be found out.

"Come here, you little bugger" or "Dere ma, y diawl bach" in Welsh, and I, as the little son of the pub, would be enveloped with invaluable kindness, chat and warmth from a dusty, chesty collier – a warmth that the world could not buy.

Some were well read – others were politically Red.

Miners kept wives and women, dogs, whippets, chickens and rabbits. My father had greyhounds, and our rented plot of land. It was my world. Kids in cities would go to parks in prams. We climbed on tractors and trailers, helped to herd the animals, and everyone pitched in with the haymaking. It was a wonderful, uncomplicated world for any youngster.

Outside the New Inn, it seemed to me that the local show brought out the valley's entire population and it was the pinnacle of my calendar in the early years. But on our (my) field we also had two Hereford Cross cows, sheep and my pony Twts. So when the school bus picked up my friends for the morning trip to Gadlys Secondary Modern in Aberdare, frequently, I wouldn't be on it. There were just too many distractions. D. Morris would be marked 'absent' on the school register. The cows and animals marked me as 'present'.

Next door were Mr and Mrs Gregory. They were a marvellous and kind couple. I would spend a great deal of my time in their bungalow, often sleeping there. It was a second home. Mr Gregory had Welsh cobs, which was a magnet for me. He was also a champion dog breeder. Mr Gregory had all the time in the world for his horses – and, therefore, me. They were true friends and neighbours. You couldn't have wished for better.

To sit in my pub home on winter nights, and hear the tales

of the coalface and the torment of hacking away, was no Enid Blyton adventure. It was real, and these men always loved the light and chat at the end of a shift. I could not wait to be a part of it. I still have the utmost admiration for colliers, and though I travelled with rugby to places on an atlas, the Rhigos chat was more important than any news bulletin. I always wanted to know what time it was in Rhigos – because I knew what was going on there, at anytime of day.

Those who left the place and returned with 'airs and accents' were given space and silence. Mind you, not many returned. It is a hard, lovely, demanding place to live. I am still there.

Hirwaun and Aberdare were fairly close to us at Rhigos, Cardiff was a distance, but as for London, Sydney and Buenos Aires – they were spots on a school atlas. Places like that did not interest me. Rhigos was my world, and the world was Rhigos.

They did in later life, of course, but my ambition as a youngster was to take on all the challenges that Rhigos and the New Inn field could provide. There were also challenges inside the pub as well. We would have to help my mother clean the tables and the dining area before going to school. It had to be spotless, or it wouldn't do. Some, like my friend Keith Griffiths, thrived in school, and he was awarded a book for being ever present throughout his schooldays. Not me – except on games days! People sent their kids to school, and if they did well, they would eventually leave Rhigos. I couldn't see the sense in that.

I have never felt envious of those who are academic. And it wasn't because I was lazy, but if there was an excuse to 'mitch' a day, or a few days for that matter, I would find something else to do. Mostly, I looked after my animals, or anybody else's animals. I could have earned a degree in 'mitching'.

You might find my name on a few boards of honour in

rugby clubhouses, but they wouldn't be for my scholastic achievements. I also knew that I could leave school on reaching my fifteenth birthday. It couldn't come soon enough. I wanted to be part of the boys – and that meant working at the nearby colliery.

Most of the family had either worked underground or kept pubs. The talk of the New Inn was my education. So my destiny was either working underground or sport.

After primary school, there was another challenge – the daily journey by bus to nearby Aberdare, and the Gadlys Secondary Modern School. This was even worse. Some days I caught the bus, some days I didn't.

I would make it on games days though, and the games teacher was Idris Evans. It was mostly football, but there were a few rugby games as well against local schools. I was placed on the wing, because I did have some speed, and could run all day if required. In the classroom I was a stoic passenger. It is no criticism of the teachers, my mind was simply elsewhere. I wasn't particularly bright, and they, the teachers, and I knew that. It was a strange thing when I sometimes met them years later. They knew me, but I didn't remember most of them.

Perhaps I should have listened more, read more and done a better job of school. But I counted the days, weeks, months and the four years up to my fifteenth birthday – when I could enrol at the NCB Apprentice Training Centre in Aberaman, learning to be an apprentice electrician for three days, and then attending school for two days. That didn't last long either.

I had no desire to be an underground miner, but, being a blacksmith, my father's work, did appeal. Perhaps it was the manual element that attracted me, because the old boys would tell you that hammering away at steel and metal all day was just as challenging as underground mining. I think those years at the colliery did build up my strength and power, and if you see a colliery blacksmith's face at work, you will see a face of graft, sweat and determination.

There was another young man in the colliery. His name was Glyn Shaw, who was possibly, in my opinion, the strongest prop ever to play for Wales. Glyn was awesome, always ready for any strength and endurance challenge. If you thought you could beat him, you would have been mistaken – lifting, carrying, heaving – and all this without any training or coaching. Unfortunately he went 'north' before reaching the pinnacle of his rugby union career. He was blond, an Adonis-style character, and that brought its problems as well. He was never short of female admirers. Glyn was a good, caring man, a great friend, and a product of the rugby mining production line.

Much later, we would travel together to the Gnoll, Neath's rugby ground, for training and games. We'd take Wayne Cornelius, a disabled man, with us in the car, make sure he was OK in his chair to watch the game, and then take to the field. It is a great friendship that has lasted to this day.

These days, questions are asked in sports quizzes about who was the last miner to play rugby for Wales. I played in an era and area where a team without miners was unheard of. Players are now prepared in gyms, weightlifting emporiums and are monitored by people with various degrees in physical education, diets, physiology and psychiatry. I do not envy these players, but the odd psychiatric visit to the old Neath dressing room would have been interesting, a rich research resource I would have thought for any young student psychiatrist! I'm not sure how many of our players would have been successfully CRB checked either. Contemporary players are assessed for everything. At my Gnoll you either had a "tidy game" or you were "bloody awful". That was it, assessment over, and can you imagine telling the likes of Twmws, Barry and Randall Davies that they were role models. This is the way the game has progressed – or has it?

Playing on a Saturday, for Rhigos, Glynneath, Neath or Wales, was an exhilarating experience. I lived for it. I do not envy the modern player at all. I envy the money they are making. But it stops there. For starters, I hardly ever trained. Colliery life took care of that. Initially, I had ambitions of being a football player. I think I had some potential as a winger, but when Twts broke my kneecap, that was just about the end of the football ambitions. It was rugby from then on – and for the next forty years or so.

Gadlys School had a few age group teams, but few opponents in that part of the world. I didn't particularly enjoy being placed on the wing either. So having made my move to the training centre, I had a decision to make. There simply weren't enough games being organised.

Life is full of crossroads and this was one of them – at least for me. Where could I go? Rhigos no longer had a rugby club, but Glynneath, Hirwaun, Seven Sisters, Cwmgwrach did. From Rhigos it is pretty much downhill to Glynneath, so that is where I went. I was fifteen and they all remember me turning up for the first training session.

I was the only one wearing white socks, because they were the only ones I had – and they were football socks too! I might have had a good career in a Welsh jersey, but the locals always ask, "Do you remember turning up at Glynneath in white socks?" I've never lived it down.

However, my mother came to the rescue. At least I would have new boots. We went to the Co-op in Aberdare and bought brown boots with studs. There was no stopping me now. I was a Glynneath player – with new boots. That was worth celebrating. So, too, was leaving school.

4

Glynneath

Tom 'Tai Cwpla' Lewis, my lifelong farmer friend, and heart and soul of Rhigos RFC, didn't think much of me as a young rugby player. He claims, because I was left handed, I couldn't pass, and had little coordination. But even he would have to confess that I was a willing pupil. I think Tom fancied himself as a bit of a Welsh selector.

What I did have were large blacksmith collier's hands, strength inherited from my father, and a good pair of lungs. There was nothing I would enjoy more than running everywhere. Tom reckons he saw me round up sheep on my own, and at an early age I was blessed with endurance, and I could run for miles.

Tom remembers once that we were repairing fences for my cattle on the rented field, and noticed that the sheep nearby were acting up and becoming very agitated. There had been a few sheep killings in the area, so we knew we had a killer dog problem.

Then we saw them, a spaniel, a retriever and a collie cross. They were about to attack the flock – my flock.

I gave chase, and they saw me. I chased them for miles as they headed for safety. But I wasn't going to give up. Tom was behind – well behind! Then I saw them head for a house, and into a shed. A lady came out of the house and closed the shed door behind them. There was a trail of blood leading to the shed – I was furious.

I do have a temper. I gave the owner a right old telling off.

Tom, I know, would have insisted on the dogs being put down, but I couldn't do that. He also reckons I must have run five miles to get to my quarry. I think it was a lot less, but Tom's version has lengthened over the years. It will be ten miles by next year!

I have always had the ability to keep going, and I have always found it hard to give in. Both Marlene and my daughter call me stubborn, and they may be right. No! Totally correct. There we are, I have confessed – in print!

Rhigos didn't have a rugby team then. It had been disbanded before the war. So when I left Gadlys School, Aberdare at fifteen, I happily joined Glynneath Youth – complete with those white socks. I was still being selected as a winger – and the game in those days dictated that the ball was never released by the halfbacks until the battle up front had been settled. I froze on the fringes! Much like today, if you play youth rugby on the wing, you have either got exceptional talents or you are just making up the numbers.

Glynneath was a hotbed of valley rugby. Just about any game in the valley was a bit of a local derby, and the rivalry was intense. There were teams everywhere – Aberaman, Hirwaun, Resolven, Cwmgwrach, Seven Sisters – but Glynneath was my choice. Colin, my younger brother, would join later.

Glynneath was also the choice of a few more Gadlys 'graduates' – Colin Veale and Martin Morris – and that helped. Truth be told, we hadn't played that many games at school. I think it was about four or five games in total. So much for rugby development! So Glynneath was a real and raw baptism from the start.

I'd already stated working as an apprentice electrician and later as a blacksmith 'striker' at Rhigos Colliery under the guidance of Glyn Prosser, a Welsh international flanker who played in a team that defeated the All Blacks in 1935. Such company! Such education!

Every day was a manual challenge with hammers, sledges or heaving timber props or some heavy metal. There wasn't much rest with Glyn and the other smithy Bryn Vaughan involved in all sorts of challenges and demands. The chat was mostly about rugby and feats of strength. It was my kind of education – and the best of grooming.

The colliery manager's son, Alwyn Martin, decided to join Glynneath Youth as well, so I was amongst people I knew.

The Glynneath club was a mixture of seasoned first-class campaigners on their way down the ranks, and a good crop of youngsters on the way up. There were no coaches, just 'captains' or people who had played for the nearby clubs of Neath, Aberavon, Maesteg and Swansea – and they all knew the game inside out, and were never too shy to pass on a few words of advice in loud voices. And, naturally, there was plenty of advice from the supporters as well. Glynneath has never been short of touchline advice.

Fitness wasn't a problem. Most were miners – challenging coal faces all week – or they were farmers, heaving and shoving every day. No gyms! No weights! These were just hard men – with reputations to enhance on Saturday afternoons and boast about that night. That was also true of most of our opponents as well – every Saturday was a battle, and I soon realised that as a youth player with white socks, I was not going to be involved that much!

So, progressing from youth, I joined the 2nds. But, more importantly I moved to number 8. Competition for a place in that side was going to be fierce. There was no shortage of candidates.

In fact, there was no shortage of candidates for any position at any club in our vicinity. Every club was a mecca for young people to play rugby. You'd never turn up with twelve, thirteen or fourteen players – at Glynneath we would leave half a dozen players behind.

It was the same situation at most other clubs. Playing rugby for fun or keeping fit was more popular than it is now.

I don't know what has gone wrong with our grass-roots rugby in Wales. We seem to cope pretty well competitively at the top level. But at the lower levels it is a mess!

There are now countless clubs who can only field one competitive team – and struggle to do that at times. Whether it is because our clubs cannot develop teams, do not have enough revenue to sustain a 2nd XV, or whether we have got it all wrong at the development stage between the school and club. Perhaps it is a combination of all of these factors – but I see some disturbing scenes on Sunday mornings with the youngsters. When teachers refused to organise Saturday morning games it had a major impact on the sport. I don't know if we have ever recovered from that.

Generally it has been left to club enthusiasts or parents to organise junior and youth sections, and despite the number of coaching courses, certificates and grades, if you haven't got willing and capable volunteers, then it is a survival battle. I don't know what needs to be done, but there are far better educated and professional people at the helm these days who should know. The gap between the professional level and ordinary club rugby is far too wide.

Edicts are sent out about criteria – the facilities you must have to wear the WRU 'brand'. But facilities cost money. Combine the wages of our professional administrators, the manager, coaches and the bill for training facilities would probably mean survival for only forty-odd clubs in Wales.

I watch some 2nd XV rugby teams where players take to the field well beyond their sell by date. Some are committee members who happen to be in the bar on a Saturday afternoon after shopping at Tesco and then volunteer to help out their club, and endanger themselves in panting between ruck and maul – and missing both.

At the higher end of the scale we have people in the WRU on huge salaries looking after our national team, but they largely ignore what is going on at the 'face'. Colliery managers were sometimes like that as well.

It happens week after week in Rhigos, where I now watch my rugby, and it makes me angry. The union send out edicts, attend dinners, appoint district officers – and the top committee men travel abroad to Dublin, South Africa, New Zealand and Australia to see whether they have got it right. They have got it wrong as far as junior rugby in Wales is concerned. They introduce a multi-million pound salary cap for our four regions, whereas some of our clubs cannot afford the electricity bill for lights!

I watch youngsters at Rhigos on a Sunday morning. Other countries, notably New Zealand, choose junior teams based on size, weight and height. We do it by age. I have seen many a junior game dominated and ruined by large couch potatoes who can run for five minutes, never giving out the ball and dominating the game. The little tots freeze on the wing in their washed and clean kits. What joy is there in that?

The papers say the top man in the WRU earns £360,000 per year. You could have bought Rhigos Colliery for that! It could have saved Tower as well. Add that sum to the inflated salaries and perks of managers, home unions and IRB committees, coaches and backroom staff – we might have saved the entire south Wales coalfield.

I'm not sure whether we need a kicking coach to bring on a tee either. They now have computers, data analysis, dieticians, pre- and post-match statistical graphs. In 1971, Carwyn James did all his analysis on the back of a Senior Service fag packet!

Clive Woodward with the British Lions employed more

people than were employed in Rhigos and Hirwaun. I just don't understand why – and I am not particularly fond of what has become, through various law changes, a very static game either. There is no room on the field for what we called a game of open rugby. They'll be wearing helmets before long.

I don't know whether we can afford all of this. The game has gone professional. But the supporters are still amateurs. We have to work our shifts in order to earn the money to pay for tickets to a game which might start at 5.30 p.m. on a Friday, 6.00 p.m. on a Saturday or 1.30 p.m. on a Sunday. Imagine trying to work colliery shifts, or any shifts for that matter, around the modern fixture schedules determined by broadcasters. I far prefer going down to watch Rhigos. They kick-off, home or away, on Saturday at 2.30 p.m. And they play for pride, not pounds.

We'd go bankrupt overnight if we had to pay the players. It has happened elsewhere, and the clubs have regretted entering the 'player market'.

We never will at Rhigos.

It was not so different when I began with Glynneath 2nd XV. We wanted to play, lived for it, there was a goal in sight, and that was playing for Glynneath and hopefully winning. There were some characters around. Idwal Griffiths was one. Idwal was a prop, and built like one too, far too large for a run at the opposition. "Let's have a scrum, boys, for God's sake!" was Idwal's panting plea throughout a game. There's no doubt he could scrummage and challenge the very best, but Idwal would roam and loiter hoping to identify the location of the next scrum.

There were few distractions either in those days. Work, play rugby and a few pints! I watch my grandchildren now, totally mesmerised 24/7 by cartoons on Sky, young kids lying on sofas and beds with Xboxes and other gadgets purring away. I don't understand it, I don't like it, and to cap it all, you can now play an international rugby game with your thumbs!

If you dropped a pass playing for Glynneath, they would tell you in no uncertain manner that you were all thumbs as well.

There were some exceptional players around the place. I mean no disrespect to any of them but, for me, the likes of Captain Bas Thomas, John Weaver, Vince Good and Lyn Tregonning were inspirational. So many of them had played or would play at a higher level. By the time I had left the youth and athletic XV to join the firsts, something special was going on at Glynneath.

It began on 2 September 1961 against Blackwood, and carried on until 13 October 1962. The second game of this epic unbeaten run was against Swansea, a team full of internationals, including Norman Gale, John Faull and Idwal Fisher. It was a missionary game of course, meant to be a celebration romp, but it ended in a 3–3 draw. Yet no one at Abernant Park complained.

There were no leagues in those days, but we played the very best around. Three points for a try then, as well.

Some of our opponents took a bit of a drubbing – Aberystwyth (31–0), Abercynon (33–3), Met Police (31–0) and only one team reached double figures against us, Abergavenny, so we were defensively tight. What mattered more, we were beating sides that had better resources, like Cardiff Athletic and Devonport Services. We went fifty-five games undefeated and won the Silver Ball by beating near neighbours Resolven 11–0. We played six games in ten days at the end of the season and won them all, and I played in forty of the forty-one games in the first season.

P 41 W 37 L 0 Points for 584 Points against 113

It was a truly combined effort with Bas Thomas at the helm and the likes of John Weaver, David Weaver, Gwyn Roberts,

Elfed Morgan, Clive Dyer, Idwal Griffiths, Dai Davies, Norman Taylor, Terry Williams, Peter Castaldi, Morton Davies, Eric Williams, Edryd Shaw, David Stacey, Martin Morris, Lyn Tregonning, John Rees and Clive Williams. I mention them all, since these guys shaped my career.

As we progressed through that season, competition for places was always intense. The committee would retire to their room on Monday night, and the clubhouse would be heaving with players and supporters, all anxious to know the selection for the next game. You'd walk away into the night if you were not in. Fortunately, I was one of the selected regulars.

And let me tell you about our motivation! Before every game, we had to sing 'The Old Rugged Cross'. It was part of our team building. No shouting or ranting – just a pre-match sing-song. Bas Thomas took us back into the changing room once, because we'd forgotten to sing our hymn.

The opposition couldn't believe it. "Chapel team, are you?" asked an opponent. Glynneath players might have been chapel goers on Sundays, but Saturdays were different! 'The Old Rugged Cross' was sung everywhere. Bas Thomas would see to that.

The team kept on winning, and the unbeaten Glynneath became known as the 'invincibles'. The run had started in the 1960/1 season and ended fifty-five games later. We were that strong that Llanelli refused to play us, but we had recorded eleven straight wins before St Luke's College, Exeter, brought it to an end down in the West Country, mainly due to the accuracy of England full back Don Rutherfod. Glynneath were equal to any club in Wales, and many argued that we should have been given first-class status.

There is no doubt that the inspiration behind our success was the ability of the captain Bas Thomas – a legend in our part of the world.

We were attracting huge crowds as well, though I suspect half of them from neighbouring villages and clubs came along hoping to see us lose! There is no love lost between these rugby playing communities.

When the unbeaten run came to an end at Exeter it was something of a relief, and only some aspects of the train journey home can be remembered.

It was a fair celebration, and we should have changed trains at Temple Meads in Bristol. But on we travelled, oblivious to that fact that we were heading for Scotland or somewhere. I still cannot explain why, but when we eventually returned home, my false teeth were missing. They were later found in Gareth Owen's blazer pocket. He was Richard Burton's nephew, but his real claim to fame in Glynneath was that he was also the mysterious custodian of my teeth!

It was not the only adventurous journey of that period. There were a few car smashes on homeward-bound journeys, and once one of the boys had to drive the bus home from Gwent – as our official driver was totally incapable of staying upright at the wheel. I hasten to add that the country had not yet been subject to breathalyser tests, nor police spot checks. If they had been around, we might have not been as 'invincible'.

Meanwhile, I was still toiling away with sledges, props, timbers and hammers, having moved to Tower Colliery, and also playing for the successful Sevens Colliery team with my old mate Dai Parker.

Our success at Glynneath attracted a fair bit of publicity in the Welsh papers, and I suppose that this ultimately caused the break-up of the 'invincibles' team.

Some of us were invited to play 'on permit' for first-class and neighbouring clubs. I played on permit for Hirwaun and Cwmgwrach. I must have made an impression at Hirwaun because when I won my first Welsh cap they made me a life member.

My first top-class game away from Glynneath was for Penarth, and then Ebbw Vale. It might be unpalatable for Neath supporters, but I also appeared four times for Llanelli as well. That Llanelli side was full of household names – Norman and Aubrey Gale, D.K. Jones, Robert Morgan, Marlston Morgan and captained by the great R.H. Williams.

I suppose I could have joined them on a permanent basis, but the M4 had not been built, or even thought of in those days, and the journey from Glynneath to Stradey Park and back was more of an expedition than a drive. Not only that, had I played another game on permit, I would have had to leave Glynneath. It was a close call.

But players were being enticed away from the club. A number of us, including myself, wanted to match ourselves against better opposition. Moving on was inevitable. But those halcyon days of the 'invincibles' will remain a great memory to those who played and watched. Max Boyce was one of them.

Lyn Tregonning and I went to play for Neath, but never 'left' Glynneath. David Weaver and Clive Dyer went to Swansea and David got his Welsh cap after only eight games. Wynford Morris joined Newport, Vince Good went to Aberavon, and that great servant of Glynneath rugby, the skipper Bas Thomas, retired.

It was the end of an exceptional period, but the friendship has always remained true. The photographs which adorn the Glynneath clubhouse vouch for that.

There was another chapter associated with my stay at Glynneath. I started courting a young hairdresser from there, who had opened her own shop in Resolven. Resolven, may I add, also had a hard, mining village rugby team, and the rivalry between Glynneath and Resolven, two neighbouring villages, was intense, if not sometimes unhealthy. The 'old foe' they were called, but sometimes the language was a bit stronger.

I got some strange looks when visiting Marlene's shop. If you were a visiting Martian you'd be all right in Resolven, but someone from Glynneath was alien. Marlene was from Glynneath, and I was playing for them.

I can't remember the exact details, but I think I proposed to her in Farraday's café in Glynneath, with a jukebox blaring in the back. I can't vouch for that, but most of our courting was done there. Perhaps I proposed at home, because I don't think I would have proposed in front of the café crowd. Wherever, it was the best move I ever made, on or off the field. We've been through thick and thin, believe you me.

I moved in to live with her and her mother in Glynneath, before moving back to Rhigos. She has been my companion, friend and backbone since then.

After joining Neath, I was invited to play in a rugby league trial at St Helens. Wigan were also pursuing me, and in those days, any suggestion that you had been associating with the 'professional game' would mean being ostracised from playing rugby union in Wales. How times have changed – union players are now earning more than league players!

But Marlene and I went 'north' with Peter Davies and his partner Jo, to visit 'friends'. I must have made an impression, since I was given a man of the match award and Wigan offered me a contract and a £2,000 fee – which to a collier was a fortune!

But neither of us were impressed with the area, or didn't fancy moving out of our comfort zone. I declined the offer. It was the only time I ever considered moving from the area.

Fortunately, they paid my petrol expenses for travelling 'up north', and I bought Marlene an engagement ring with the proceeds. I am indebted to rugby league for that – 'the Wigan engagement ring'!

5

Neath

Introduction by the late Brian Thomas

WE'D HEARD ABOUT him. Anyone who scores twenty-two tries in an unbeaten Glynneath team is bound to get talked about. It was said that he was a bit of a 'poacher', which is that uncanny ability that can't be taught, to be in the right place at the right time.

What we were not prepared for was his fitness levels. His running ability was the talk of the valley. I'd never met anyone or anything like him.

At Neath in pre-season we used to have these gruelling runs up the mountains above the town – or up to Tonna and Aberdulais and back – a six-mile lung puller. People like me used to dread this pre-season stuff. I was not built like Seb Coe, and certainly not built for running long distances.

Dai would be back from the run, having had a shower, whereas some of us would only be halfway up the mountain.

He didn't drink much either!

If he did, then look out! He had a habit of throwing things into swimming pools. Not things, I mean people!

I remember him and John Lloyd hitting the bottle or Cava juice on tour in Fiji when the Welsh team were being visited by the king and the British high commissioner. The king was a bit of a character, since he'd already told us that the first

Christian missionaries to Fiji were Welsh Baptists – and "very tasty they were too"!

Dai and John, at the end of the tour, were well into the Cava juice and thought it might be fun if they chucked the WRU management team – the whole lot of them – into the hotel pool, which they did! I can tell you that the king was much amused by this baptism as well.

His strength, honed from banging away as a blacksmith striker at Pandy and Tower Colliery was legendary. He brought his colliery lifting techniques to the rugby field – and if anyone was in the way, including his own players, then look out! Sometimes he was a blasted nuisance – just getting in the way.

I had mastered a mauling technique, of grasping the ball, and using my back to turn around, drop to my knees, and then feed back. All Dai wanted to do was lift me back up again! We had words about that!

You couldn't get the ball from him if he didn't want you to have it. His arms and upper body, for a man his weight and height, was phenomenal. From painful experience he didn't hold back in training sessions either.

In many ways, Dai altered our approach to player recruitment at Neath.

I don't ever recall trying to motivate Dai. Some of the others had to be told what was required of them, and sometimes had to be reminded during a game as well. But not our Dai. He knew what he had to do, and he did it throughout the game. No fuss, he was sometimes at the point of breakdown before it happened. If I had tried to motivate him, he'd probably have pouted and gone into a shell. I don't know, because I never tried.

We wanted more people like Dai, who worked in demanding physical day jobs, and suddenly Neath was full of miners, steelworkers and farmers – hard men. Glyn Shaw was another one.

Years later, as Neath's manager, I used the same recruitment approach in building Neath's most successful team in the history of the club. The Neath front row of John Davies, Kevin Phillips and Brian Williams were all from farming stock.

Dai's only problem was getting to any place on time – apart from rucks and mauls! I knew he would be there, because he didn't let anyone down. But three minutes to kick-off, which it was at times, was cutting it a bit fine.

The late Brian Thomas
Captain of Neath

*   *   *

I would either work a shift or tend to my animals on a Saturday morning, which nearly always meant that we were late leaving Rhigos for Neath and the Gnoll. Kick-off at Neath was 3.15 p.m. every Saturday afternoon. The distance between Rhigos and the Gnoll is nineteen miles.

Invariably, Tom Tai Cwpla and Dai Pumps would be there waiting, impatiently, for me, engine running, as we left about ten to three in Tom's Singer Vogue or my Ford Cortina. I would change and drive the car as much as I could, leaving Tom to do the parking when we got to the Gnoll, and I would run through the changing room and onto the field doing up my boot laces.

The other players had been there for a while, banging doors, stamping the floor, shouting at each other – that was not for me – I didn't care for those motivational talks. If you can't motivate yourself you shouldn't be there. Besides, I would have been thinking about the game for days.

Of course, my lateness and my fidgeting became legendary, and it would send captains and coaches up the wall – it gave Tom and, later, Glyn Shaw a few grey hairs as well – especially if I was driving. This was especially true of away games – because Tom, Dai and myself went everywhere by car. We were inseparable. We drove to London Welsh, Coventry and Dublin, and, given the chance, they and I would have driven to Argentina and Canada as well!

We all had a fondness for cars. I remember when I had a two-seater MGB. That was great fun, but then Marlene got pregnant with Helen, and three into two didn't go. Even the Gadlys secondary modern education taught me that, and the car had to go. It was my pride and joy. But then, so is Helen.

I am convinced that if I had been one of those who could get wound up by an emotive speech or a call to arms, I wouldn't have enjoyed the game – I'd be too nervous. I remember Ron Jones of Coventry before a Wales match. He'd be up half the night wrenching his soul, no sleep, all because of nerves.

And we did have some 'call to arms' merchants. Not on a Clive Rowlands, Cwmtwrch scale, but not far behind. So if I did happen to be early, it would be a mistake, and I would find something to do. If there was a bookie in the vicinity, then that was ideal, especially in Cardiff on international days. There'd be supporters in there as well, always asking "Shouldn't you be changed by now, Dai?" or "Pulled out, have you, Dai?" That was something I rarely did – even when injured, or suffering from a bloody kick from a horse.

When joining, I was aware that Neath had just lost their number 8 John Davies to rugby league, a superb player, so there was a place up for grabs in the back row.

Competition for a first-team place would be intense but, together with the Glynneath 'grooming' and some limited experience of first-class rugby at Stradey, Ebbw Vale and Penarth, I thought I could hold my own.

But, looking around that changing room and seeing the likes of Brian Thomas, Randall, Peter, Barry and Dai Davies, Alan Butler, Ron Waldron, Morlais Williams, Mike Thomas,

Alan Dix, John Dodd, Wilson Lauder, Grahame Hodgson, Glen Ball, Gwyn Ashby, Martyn Davies – I knew I would have my work cut out. So would the opposition. These were names I had revered, and read about. Neath, to us in Rhigos, Cwmgwrach, Tonna, Resolven and Glynneath was the pinnacle.

I was also shocked and taken aback by the fanaticism of the Neath fans. I'd experienced big crowds and great support at Glynneath, but there was something more extreme about the Gnoll crowd. The pitch was surrounded by iron railings, and the noise when young boys would find something to rattle against the railings as the team took to the field is a memory for ever. The opposition, in their dark changing room, knew that they were at the Gnoll, especially from the 'shed' end, and the intimidation would start well before the first whistle.

It was the beginning of a love affair – and over the years the only position I didn't play in the pack for Neath was hooker! Yes, I even propped for them against Oxford!

There were 'rewards' for this kind of commitment. Arthur Griffiths was the Neath secretary and in charge of expenses. We had to line up at the end of the game outside his little office, just like school, to receive our allowance, as long as you promised not to tell anyone else, especially the next player waiting outside, what you were receiving! I honestly believed that everyone received the same, and Twmws wouldn't tell you anyway. Arthur was that naive, but a Neath legend – for all his work over the years, not his charitable nature. During my first season I received 10s petrol allowance, 50p. I suppose in today's language – the price of a stamp. In my second season the allowance rose to £1. At least it was something, and you could buy four gallons of petrol for £1 in those days.

Arthur also had battles with Brian Thomas. Twmws insisted on having two of the Gnoll floodlights turned on for training. Arthur, who lived in a house overlooking the Gnoll would send his wife down to tell Twmws to turn one of them off. You can imagine Brian's response. The professional era was light years away from those days – no pun intended.

Years later with the Welsh team, Bill Clement was the WRU secretary, and here was another penny pincher. He would roam the Aberavon car park to see and check which players were sharing lifts, something that Glyn Shaw and I did on a regular basis. He would then halve our petrol allowance. We were training for Wales! What a bargain he had with the London Welsh boys, when six or seven of them who would come down to Wales crammed into two cars!

Bill Clement may have been a scrooge, but he was always a gentleman. Yet, if you didn't have a receipt, he wouldn't pay. Phil Bennett found that out when he claimed for a meal in the motorway services after beating England at Twickenham. No receipt – no pay.

Even worse was the scrutiny and hypocrisy of the union. At the end of the season you were asked to play in all sorts of invitational games. I'd never turn down an invitation, but it was, after all, your time and decision to play. Sometimes, but rarely in Wales, you'd be offered a few quid for petrol. If the match was reported in the newspapers, there'd be a call from the union, asking us to forward the money to them.

These were the same people who used to travel to away matches – with their wives – with all expenses paid. I did note that in a few charity or international XV programmes, that A.N. Other, S.O. Else and A. Forward featured in most games. This wasn't tax evasion, this was WRU and Bill Clement evasion.

And you did wonder where all the revenue from home matches in Cardiff went.

I know things were different then. However, the union

always had full houses at the Arms Park, and those faithful supporters with their weekly wages would buy tickets for a lot more money than we were receiving for our petrol allowance. In that respect, I don't things changed a great deal until the dawn of the professional era. Then it went bonkers!

I had always been a stickler for fair and hard play. I still am. I couldn't stand foul tactics. There were others at Neath who were of a different persuasion and chapel. Our skipper, Brian Thomas, had a reputation for being hard and aggressive, and though I saw him do some pretty terrible things, he received far more punishment than he gave out. Brian's back after some games resembled a well-used golf course. Yet, he never complained. "Don't do it, Brian" I used to shout at him, but I was invariably too late, and the deed had been done.

This, from a man with a Cambridge degree, who was to become boss of the Port Talbot steelworks and the scourge of any journalist or paper that dared to mention anything unsavoury about Neath's 'style of play' or intimidation. Brian raised thousands of pounds over the years for rugby injury charities in pursuing or threatening defamation cases against the papers. He even took on Tony Lewis, former cricket captain of England, but also a rugby correspondent for *The Telegraph*. What is more – he's from Neath! Many of the cases were settled before they got to court. Clever man was Brian, and I was glad to have him as a great friend and a supporter of Rhigos, the birthplace of his mother.

Yet, I can remember one incident quite vividly. I should, because it was my first game for the Welsh All Blacks in 1963. St Luke's College, Exeter, were the visitors, and not the force that they had once been. It was a side of young talented students, keen to impress with their running skills. They had no hope of matching our pack, and Barry Davies, formidable in every sense of the word, decided to give them an all-embracing Gnoll welcome – because he was out to enjoy himself.

I could see what was going on. He was 'sledging' them at every line-out. I asked him to stop, but he wouldn't. Why should he listen to a rookie upstart? So I told Brian, the captain, "Twmws, tell him to stop – they are only youngsters". Barry again ignored Brian's request. "Barry, if you don't stop sledging them, I will give you one myself" said Brian, and at the next line-out, he did.

So a fight broke out between Brian and Barry on the St Luke's '25', with the game some sixty yards away.

Eventually it finished, with Brian accusing me of being the instigator. "Your bloody fault" he ranted, and worse still, we drew the game 3–3. Sadly the great man has gone, and I have yet to come to terms with that.

But teams did fear coming to the Gnoll, much as they did later when going to Pontypool. The fanatical Neath supporters' 'shed' behind the goalposts at the Gnoll was no place for a neutral. Three thousand of them, packed like sardines behind the goalposts, all on first-name terms with each other.

There was no hiding the fact that the intention was to intimidate opposing teams, by making the Gnoll an unforgiving fortress.

Don't forget, prior to leagues being introduced, we played Swansea, Llanelli and Aberavon four times a season, and they were all pretty tribal affairs. Nothing like a bit of Welsh rugby integration! There was an unofficial *Western Mail* championship table, and later a Floodlight Alliance League, but, in reality, bragging rights were sorted out by the local derbies – and also by individuals protecting their 'hard' reputations.

It wasn't unusual to play some fifty games in a season, and Neath played as many additional 'missionary' games with the local junior clubs as they could cram in.

I remember Llanelli turning up for one of those wet Wednesday night fixtures, and such was our reputation, Llanelli only just managed to scrape a side together, due to some notable late withdrawals. Phil Bennett was their captain, and I know that Phil even now remembers the night only too well. Brian snorted down at Phil for the toss, just to make sure that our intentions were clear!

Hereford bull looking down on a Welsh cob, with a nervous Welsh lamb of a referee in the middle!

We gave them a physical drubbing up front, and then I saw Phil half-tackled and he was inevitably due for some Neath indelible footwear on the floor. I jumped on his back, and told him to stay down. I took the studs meant for him, because I didn't believe in that sort of game.

That game rendered the Llanelli changing room more akin to a casualty ward. It was a filthy match, and Phil's recollection of it was being totally bemused by our full back Grahame Hodgson complaining after the game of a stud mark on his back.

Worse was to follow – Cardiff suspended fixtures with Neath for four years. I remember that game. It was a match at the Arms Park. The plan was to stop the Cardiff halfbacks, Gareth and Barry. It was not a pretty sight, since our pack, if they got hold of them, would ruck over them, making sure their presence was felt, and then ruck back over them again for a reminder. It was not my scene at all, but I was a minority vote. Barry stalked off saying "If that is rugby football, I am finished". I am not sure whether Gareth ever played Neath at the Gnoll after that game either. Few relished a visit to the Gnoll. It was an intimidating place with intimidating occupants. But we could play good rugby.

Those early seasons were for me a major awakening to the higher demands of the game. Grahame Hodgson, one of the finest full backs to grace the game, organised the sessions. But the one thing I couldn't stand was being organised – I just wanted to play. I couldn't understand graphs and statistics – you don't play rugby on paper!

I now watch the TV pundits who have the support of replays, gadgets, graphics and goodness-know-how-many computers to analyse every line-out, ruck or incident.

They should know better because on the field it is helter-skelter. The game isn't played in slow motion, you almost don't have time to think.

I am disappointed that so many former internationals so quickly become analysts and critics, critical of their contemporaries. It is a hard enough path getting to the position of being an international player. The last thing you want to hear, I would say, is one of your former team-mates having a go at you on the basis of a television and computer replay. Thank God they were not that sophisticated in my day. Even worse is the employment on television of players' agents as pundits. The *Western Mail* on a Monday was bad enough for us lot, but if you had played badly, you'd be told in fairly graphic detail in punter language before you reached the sanctuary of the Angel Hotel steps.

Our Neath 'coach', Grahame Hodgson, was a teacher, and had always prepared his training sessions methodically. We did have an exchange of words on one night (over what I can't remember), but it had been one classroom talk too many, and I walked off. You didn't need a degree or a clipboard to work out what Neath rugby was all about.

Quite simply, the pack came first, and that was understood by all, especially with some of the physical merchants we had at Neath.

Brain Thomas was in charge of that department. The backs could have the ball to play with when superiority and personnel had been settled up front – and only then.

My role, initially at number 8, was to follow the ball, offer support and be the first to the tackle, ruck or maul. When we wanted to, we could compete with any side, at any level.

There was a lot of talent in that dark dressing room. It wasn't really big enough to cater for us all, and I can remember some of us tiptoeing along the benches, since one of our lads suffered from acute and stinking athlete's foot. That would have amused the opposition.

It was a 'Bible-black' dressing room, very close and intimidating. I can still smell it now. Not pleasant.

Each one had his way of preparing for a game, and with the likes of Twmws, Randal, Peter, Barry and Dai Davies you were never short of good robust challenging language. There was also humour. And when Dai Parker joined from Swansea, all 5' 2" of him, it was more like the London Palladium.

But, my, there were some good players in that changing room: Wilson Lauder, Norman Rees, Alan Mages, Lyn Tregonning, Walter Williams, John Dodd, Morlais Williams, Ron Waldron, Glen Ball, Alan Dix, Grahame Hodgson, Glyn Shaw, Martyn Davies – there was a constant stream of quality players who wanted to play for Neath. Not a bad one amongst them.

In those days the gap between first class and second class was not as wide as it is now between regional rugby and junior sides. So for midweek games which were part of the Floodlit Alliance, Neath could always depend on the village sides around – Crynant, Seven Sisters, Briton Ferry, Neath Athletic, Cimla or Glynneath for a supply of good players. There were far too many games then, not for me, but since the introduction of floodlights in Wales in 1957 at Cross Keys of all places, fixture secretaries and treasurers would cram the weeks with games. I used to enjoy the alliance games, because the points system was based on tries scored. "Use it or lose it" the modern referee shouts. We didn't have to be told in those days.

It is difficult, and I would say impossible or futile to compare today's game, the laws and the structure of it to that of some forty years ago. To start with, following Rhigos as I do, I cannot understand or believe how some teams and clubs who were on the Neath fixture list have fallen behind.

Penarth used to host the Barbarians on Good Friday but are now a division three club. So too are Dunvant, who had a remarkable rise to the top tier of Welsh rugby, with D-D-D Dai Dunvant at the helm. Maesteg once hosted the New Zealand Maoris, and are currently no longer in the premiership division. Same for Glamorgan Wanderers, Newbridge, Ebbw Vale, Treorchy and Tredegar. It is an incredible transformation.

Believe you me, in my time, a wet Wednesday night game against Maesteg, Newbridge, Ebbw Vale or Glamorgan Wanderers was no picnic.

These were immensely proud clubs and feeders to the Welsh XV. Ebbw Vale produced the finest in Denzil Williams, Clive Burgess and Arthur Lewis; Chico Hopkins and Alan Rees came from Maesteg; Dennis Hughes from Newbridge. Huge talents.

You couldn't afford to take weakened midweek sides to these places.

Naturally, the games against Cardiff, Newport, Swansea and Llanelli were as intense as any international. I would also, during my time, place Bridgend, Pontypridd, Aberavon and Pontypool in that category as well.

I'm not sure why, but it was always Cardiff we wanted to beat.

I had joined Neath in March 1963. The captain was a Seven Sisters man, Morlais Williams, who would have won several caps for Wales but for the presence of the late Norman

Gale, down the road at Llanelli. Morlais, John Dodd and Ron Waldron were picked en bloc for a Welsh trial, which shows the high regard they attracted. Only Ron was capped, and later he was to coach Wales.

This was a major elevation to higher skill levels and commitment. John Dodd, who followed Morlais, was a superb captain for three seasons, and with the likes of Dai Davies, my 'best man', Randall, his brother, Peter Davies my 'agent up north', we were never short of muscle, belief or mischief. It was a superb education.

It wasn't all about the pack. There was not a better full back around than Grahame Hodgson. He could handle anything, and his kicking and catching under the old laws was immaculate.

But the man beginning to show his influence on all matters was Twmws. One Brian Thomas, and a power house in the Welsh and Neath scrum. He would not take a backward step, and he later became captain of one of the most successful and feared Neath sides; his call of "On, on and on" is still with me.

Twmws was also a reader of men, which is just as well, because he generally left me alone to do the things I was supposed to do: follow, set up and be there. I never understood him half the time anyway! But most times the language was more Cimla than Cambridge, and I understood that.

He was never aloof. The Neath changing room was no literary society – BAs meant 'Bugger All'. BSc stood for British Steel Co. – one of the main employers in the area at that time, and outside the changing room it was "Neath, Neath, Neath" or once, when one of our boys had been accused of biting, "Teeth, Teeth, Teeth".

The pack was made of hard men, and in November 1963, Neath and Aberavon combined to meet the All Blacks at the Talbot Athletic ground. It was to be my first major match.

The All Blacks party included legendary players such as Ken Gray, the Meads brothers, Tremain, Lochore, the captain Wilson Whineray and, at 15, the great Don Clarke. It was for these moments I had waited. I could not believe I was on the same field as them.

We gave them a stern test, but a late try by Ken Gray and a conversion by Clarke gave the tourists the honours by 11–6. Though a relative newcomer, I had not been overwhelmed by the power of the All Blacks. I could stay, I could compete, and maybe… one day?

The Gnoll ground was being developed and there were additional games to celebrate the new stand, floodlights and one of the memorable achievements was creating a ground record by winning thirty-five games out of forty-four played, and winning the Snelling Sevens.

It got even better the next season with Grahame Hodgson as skipper: we won thirty-eight games and extended the ground record – it was now Fortress Gnoll.

Twmws had been capped by Wales as well, and I have to mention his one and only Welsh try against Scotland in twenty-one appearances for his country. I won't mention the length of his run to the line, but with Norman Gale and Brian Price supporting him, it wasn't a sprint!

There was a huge momentum around the Neath changing room. Again, as a combined Neath and Aberavon team, we lost to the touring Australians by 9–3, but Neath won the 1967 Welsh championship with only one defeat against Cardiff. Though that one defeat didn't go down well, we were crowned *The Sunday Telegraph*'s champions of Britain.

That team was probably the most complete of Neath teams in my experience. There was no budging the front row boys of John Dodd, Morlais Williams, Ron Waldron and the late Walter Williams. Behind them, you had the splendid weight and commitment of Barry Davies and Brian. And the back row included Grahame Hodgson's prodigy from Llantwit Major and Brynteg Comprehensive School, Wilson Lauder of Scotland. Wilson had already played for the Welsh schoolboys, but being born in Thornton Fife, his choice at senior level, thank goodness, was to opt for Scotland. An excellent player, extremely athletic and durable, great in an all black Neath jersey, but a pain in the blue of Scotland.

Behind the pack, we had the late Martyn Davies at scrum half and, but for the reign of Gareth Edwards and Chico Hopkins, could have worn the Welsh jersey. Keith Evans was a very competent outside half, and in Brian Davies and Glen Ball we had a superb centre pairing of guile and speed. The back three of the late Howard Rees and Hywel Williams were direct finishers, and behind Grahame Hodgson was a rock. We were a formidable team, and on every final whistle I couldn't wait for the next game.

Years later under the captaincy of Kevin Phillips, Neath produced another all-conquering side on Ron Waldron's coaching watch. There has been many a time when arguments have raged as to which Neath team would have come on top had we been able to play against each other. I shall leave that one to the Neath pundits.

But there were a few other significant events during that season. I had to drop out of the Neath team for a game against Bridgend. I was 'rested' as I had been picked for my first cap.

The second event was the appearance of a scrum half from Briton Ferry. Wilson Lauder was 6' 2" but this fella from Metal Box, down the road, was 5' 2". His name was Dai Parker, probably the smallest halfback in the history of first-class rugby in Wales. We won a few trophies together, and I always told the blazers to give the 'little one' the winners' cup or trophy.

Dai was a scrum half, but could also play at 10 as well.

Those who dismissed him did so at their peril, because he was a Metal Box of tricks. My job was to shield him, since he was an obvious target for opposing back rows. He didn't need that much protection, because he could turn on a sixpence, had an amazingly accurate boot and was a real snapper, shouting at people twice his size and double his weight. He was very cheeky and mischievous. I remember him telling a bus driver after a game against Newport at Rodney Parade "OK, driver, all on board, we can go now". And off we went leaving half the Neath team behind.

He was, and still is, the centre of attention wherever he goes, either as a charity event organiser, a stand-up comedian or just enjoying the 'craic'. He does light up a room. I am not sure how many functions he has been asked to attend and perform at. What I do know is that he doesn't charge – especially for charities and rugby clubs. He is that kind of genuine guy, and I am proud to have him as a great friend, driver and diary keeper. His contacts book should be given to the National Library in Aberystwyth. Dai knows just about everybody.

Dai shared the number 9 Neath jersey with the late Martyn Davies. If Martyn played, Dai would revert to outside half, but you could still hear him chirping away. I've never known such a bundle of energy and good humour.

We played together in the colliery 'sevens' tournaments, although he was a 'guest' as were a few others. We played in the 'Snelling' Sevens for Neath and won it at the Arms Park – it was the main tournament in Wales at the time. There's a great picture of him holding the shield on the shoulders of Wilson Lauder and Norman Rees. He's smiling, but I bet he was pretty uncomfortable being that much off the ground. He was always the same. But I have to admit that the colliery sevens and some of the valley invitational competitions, for pure enjoyment, were the best. We were often short of players, and anyone walking from a shift, with time to spare, was bundled into the car or van, kitted out and given a short lesson on sevens technique. Inevitably, our invited mercenaries played on the wing.

The Neath record of that 1966/7 season shows that we played some fifty-five club games, including a game for the combined Neath and Aberavon team against Australia which we lost 9–3.

I was dropped by Wales for the game against Brian Lochore's All Blacks, with a back row of Dennis Hughes, John Jeffrey and John Taylor selected. But I did have a crack at them playing for West Wales at St Helens, where we were skippered by Clive Rowlands.

I really shouldn't have played because I was suffering from some severe bruising of my rib cage, but Rowlands, the charmer, insisted I was required, so I was strapped up. Not quite the condition to meet the world's best and strongest rugby team.

The side was coached by the late Carwyn James, and I think that this was the only time he and Clive combined. Clive, Delme and I were the only capped players in the side, with the All Blacks being able to field Kel Tremain, Ian Kirkpatrick, Colin Meads and Sid Going at scrum half. We held our own, and my back row colleagues Morrie Evans and Bobby Wanbon gave their best. We were not intimidated and didn't do too badly, losing by 14–21. I was never convinced that combined or invitational teams stood much chance against touring sides. Our performance I think inspired Newport, who beat them a few weeks later.

The All Blacks, Wallabies and Springboks always had the advantage of being together for weeks of training, same as the Lions on tour, whereas we were reliant on limited sessions. I am sure that the Neath side of that time would have given the other All Blacks a run for their money.

It was my first introduction to Clive as a captain, orator and motivator. Little did I know then that he would play such an influential role in my career. Quite a few Rowlands' speeches would have been heard by the time I finished playing.

If you could bottle Clive's passion for Wales and rugby and sell it, we wouldn't have a drug problem in Wales – we'd be on a constant high. I was raised in Rhigos, and so Clive would remind me of the exploits of Dic Penderyn and the Merthyr riots. Playing against England would bring in the 'English' coalmine owners who had exploited Wales. He had an angle for everyone, and if he found a nationalistic theme, a figure or an historical event symbolising Welsh defiance from the player's locality, he would use it. God knows what he did with John Taylor.

Neath is the oldest club in Wales, and recent reports suggest that rugby was played in Neath, at Court Herbert, even a few years before the club was started in 1871. Strangely though, and no one really knows why, the club wasn't present when the Welsh Rugby Union was established. Even stranger because the founding meeting was held in Neath, at the Castle Hotel.

So, with three years to go before our centenary, there was a committee working hard preparing for the celebrations.

For us as players, we knew that year would be something special. It was.

Glen Ball took over the captaincy of the club, a player of huge ability, but unfortunately although he toured with Wales and me in Argentina, he was denied a Welsh cap, which he thoroughly deserved. Glen was a player's player.

Glen was also a product of Neath Athletic, a club that was instigated by the legendary Rees Stephens. He and others had the vision back in the late 1940s that Neath's youngsters needed a youth team. From that acorn grew Neath Athletic, and as the senior club approached the centenary, it was worth noting the immense contribution of Neath Athletic as a conveyor belt of talent, such as: Barri Davies, Dai Parker, Alan Butler, Ron Waldron, Martyn Davies, Walter Williams, John Bevan and Brian Rees, as well as Glen.

Neath Athletic's drive for full WRU status and financial stability also meant a few invitational games being organised. I used to love these games, because the results were relatively unimportant but the performance was.

Twmws put together a Neath XV to play an international XV, and later an invitational XV took on a combined Neath/ Swansea XV. Huge crowds, and great fun.

Alas, the professional era does not allow such celebration games, and the rugby scene is that much poorer for it. True, Welsh Charitables RFC are able to field good sides for worthy causes, but in my day, I would probably play half a dozen invitational matches at the end of the season; sometimes more.

Some of the smaller clubs depended on such occasions as fund-raisers. Can you imagine the Blues, Ospreys, Scarlets or Dragons releasing their players for a social run around? Without such games, I am not sure whether Rhigos RFC would have been reborn.

Neath's centenary 1971/2 fixture list was a rugby galaxy, and a year to savour. Martyn Davies had taken over the captaincy, and included in a packed season were the Irish Wolfhounds, the Barbarians, a 'Snelling Sevens' XV, a West Wales XV, and a WRU Presidents XV. Add those to the domestic weekly battles and the newly created WRU Challenge Cup competition and there was hardly time for the jerseys to dry.

Even in celebratory matches you couldn't afford to relax. In the Barbarians back row, England's Peter Dixon was my opposite number, a man who was selected for the 1971 Lions. And who should be in the WRU Presidents XV back row? None other than Mervyn Davies, John Taylor and Tommy David. There was always a point to prove.

I'm not one for the dinners, but the Barbarians after-match function held at the historic Castle Hotel was memorable, if only for the menu.

I think the Welsh Tourist Board should ask some of our leading hotels to adopt it. There the good and mighty of the rugby world sat down to a meal of:

Llanelli mushroom soup or Swansea fruit juice

#

Neath roast beef
Aberavon horseradish sauce
Maesteg roast potatoes
Bridgend boiled potatoes
Glamorgan Wanderers garden peas
Penarth cauliflower
Pontypridd carrots

#

Cardiff apple pie
Newport fresh cream

#

Ebbw Vale assorted cheeses
Abertillery rolls
Pontypool biscuits
Cross Keys butter

#

and, finally,

#

Newbridge coffee

There was some serious business to attend to as well during the centenary season. It was exhausting to start with, fifty-seven games in total, and I played in forty-six of them.

We knew we couldn't sustain the performance level required to win the unofficial championship. Our centenary season also coincided with the growing emergence of London Welsh, a team of internationals, class players who only played once a week, whereas we, in some weeks, were playing three times.

But the introduction of the WRU Challenge Cup did give us a focus and, as we progressed through the rounds with fairly unconvincing wins against Cefneithin, Ebbw Vale and Cardiff in the semi-final, the prospect of silverware in the centenary trophy room did concentrate minds and effort.

Our opponents in the inaugural final were Llanelli, captained by Barry Llewelyn, and a team featuring my mate Delme Thomas and a back line with Phil Bennett, Ray Gravell and Roy Mathias on board.

We won that inaugural final, 15–9. It was the fifth time we had played them that season – and our first win! It didn't matter to us that only 12,000 turned up to watch it. It was a centenary year achievement.

However, the centenary took its toll. It had been a marvellous year, but as so often happens, the following seasons were just like the morning after. Llanelli, and later Pontypool became the dominant clubs.

A number of our players left, some retired and a couple went 'north'. There were still glimpses of rare individual brilliance, notably by a young winger, Elgan Rees, who was a nightmare to follow, but inspirational to watch.

Perhaps a measure of how far we had fallen from our high standards was a match where we once again combined with Aberavon to meet the touring All Blacks in 1973. Llanelli had already beaten them early on, in that legendary 9–3 Stradey Park fixture.

But our combined side was no match for them later on and we were swamped 43–3. The decline was noted by Brian Thomas, who had already retired. It was Twmws and Ron Waldron who began plotting the revival of Neath. It was to take time.

Personally, I was being challenged for my Welsh position by Tommy David, who had impressed everyone with his performance for Llanelli against New Zealand. He had also made a fine contribution to that memorable opening try scored by the Barbarians against the All Blacks.

Tommy was a robust ball carrier, not only for Llanelli but also for his home-town club Pontypridd.

That Llanelli side was full of talent, and marshalled by Carwyn James. He had focused on bringing victory to the Scarlets on their home patch after the 1971 Lions tour. Their recruitment of J.J. Williams from Bridgend, Chico Hopkins from Maesteg and Tommy from Pontypridd showed months of meticulous planning. Our effort as a combined Neath and Aberavon side was embarrassing.

It was also a barren period for Wales. Then, towards the end of that season, it happened. My first-class career with Neath and Wales came to an abrupt end.

I had played thirty-four games over eight seasons for Wales and scored six tries in all. Being part of a team that won the Five Nations Championship three times, two Triple Crowns and a Grand Slam was an achievement for us – and a source of pride. Even more so was playing 414 games for Neath.

6

Wales

Introduction by Clive Rowlands

HE WAS UNIQUE. He never gave less than 100 per cent. Dai had a massive engine and an instinct for the game that no coach can teach.

He wasn't that tall – 6' I think, and was lighter than John Taylor. I don't think he was ever 14st – even now, just an ounce over 13st in his socks. But he was as hard as nails, with big hands and had an inner strength and will that you couldn't measure. As for heart and commitment – beyond!

Ray Williams was the WRU coaching adviser in my days, and he suggested that we consider, like the southern hemisphere, playing left and right flankers instead of the traditional 'blind and open'. There was some resistance to this at club level, but I knew that in Dai Morris, Mervyn Davies and John Taylor I had the perfect combination. Both Dai and John were quick and could add other dimensions to the game plan. Dai played number 8 for Neath, but he was a natural flanker.

So, with the ball going right or left, one of them would track every ball carrier.

These days they go to Poland for preparation weeks. We went to Aberavon beach on Sundays! That was cold enough!

But I remember telling Dai at one of those beach sessions, once the ball is passed out, you chase on the inside. We lined the three of them up against the Welsh backs to give chase – Dai, Mervyn and John Taylor.

So there I'd be, with Gareth taking the ball from Brian Price from the unopposed line-out and me shouting at Dai, "Chase inside!" Then Barry would have it and the same instruction to Dai, "Inside! Stop the inside break!"

Along the backs he'd loop in and out. "Inside, inside!"

The tide had come in a fair bit and I hadn't noticed, so when our wing Maurice Richards got hold of the ball, he was well into the waves, and he decided to go on the outside. Dai was alongside him, and floored him! Tidal wave!

I don't know how many dinners and presentations I have been to, where those great players and team have been honoured. At each one, you would have Gareth, Barry, Phil, J.P.R., John 'Sid' Dawes, but the one question always asked is: "Is Dai Morris here?"

That says it all. He was the people's hero.

Clive Rowlands
Welsh coach

*   *   *

I was working at Tower Colliery when I was first picked for Wales. I think my mother took the call at our pub, the New Inn in Rhigos. There wasn't much fuss or publicity, but I had to go down to Glynneath to have my picture taken for the newspapers. My mother paid for it. That was about it! No press conferences as they have today. Just a knowing nod from a few neighbours who had heard the news on the Rhigos grapevine.

You can't imagine the pride. The glow from Rhigos would have been spotted by aliens. The New Inn was full that night!

Rhigos would make the news! Just in case you are wondering – Rhigos hardly ever made the news, except for when we have snow drifts!

My mother supported me in every way. She would come to the Gnoll games, make sure my stuff was ready, and when that call came to the pub, I knew she was dead proud. My father would have been proud too, but in a different quiet way. He didn't come to games as frequently as my mother: being a publican and a colliery blacksmith filled his hours. It didn't mean he was less supportive, but someone had to keep the pub going.

I knew I might have a chance one day, since I had been a travelling reserve for a couple of games. There were no replacements or 'bench' in those days, so as a reserve you attended the training sessions, went with the team, but basically you were excess baggage. That was so annoying.

My first 'trial' experience at Llanelli was frustrating as well. It was a very wintry weekend, and the game was at Stradey Park.

Tom Tai Cwpla was driving, but we had left it a little late – again! The roads were icy, but we ploughed on. When we arrived in Llanelli, the traffic queues were enormous, and I had to get out of the car and make a run for the changing room. Not the first time I had done that, and certainly not the last!

Ken Grindle reckons I could change into a rugby kit faster than any stripper could take their clothes off! How he knows that, I don't know.

I shouldn't have bothered running that day since Stradey Park was frozen and unplayable, so the game was switched to the nearby Llanelli Grammar School. Thousands on the touchlines! Just like a Rhigos village game – apart from the crowds! Not quite the stage I had expected, but I did score three tries, so I assume I was noted.

The great Alun Pask was in charge of the Welsh number 8 jersey and, sadly, because of a bereavement in his family, he pulled out of the French game in 1967. I was called up for Paris for my first cap! I had never been abroad. And that, believe you me, was a bit of a problem. I didn't have a passport! Mam went to find one in Aberdare and then Newport. It wasn't easy. The easiest part was being picked.

The WRU sent me a card to ask about my availability and travel requirements. There was a question on this card as to whether I would prefer travelling to Paris by plane or by boat. I wasn't too keen on flying, though I'd never been in a plane, so given the option I marked the card indicating that I would prefer going by sea.

It didn't dawn on me that I would be the only player to go for this option. So I faced having to make my own travel arrangements. Me? Talk about an innocent abroad? There hadn't been any foreign trips from Gadlys School. Furthest we ever went to was Barry Island! And I'm not absolutely sure I went.

It wasn't quite that bad, because I received directions and my tickets for the ferry in the post, as well as the train tickets to London. Then I was told I would have company as well. Rees Stephens, one of the selectors, a Neath and Wales legend, would come with me. I wouldn't have known what to do with the underground in London, nor the other end in Calais. So off we went on the big adventure. Train to Cardiff, and then to London and on to Dover. I was a wreck before getting to France.

We caught a train from Calais to Paris, and then a taxi to the team hotel. There were some Welsh supporters on the train, but no one bothered me. I assume no one thought that their fellow passenger was playing for Wales! They seemed to be seasoned travellers, so I was happy that we were heading in the right direction.

The match was on April Fool's Day, 1967, and it was also a first cap for a young 19-year-old called Gareth Owen Edwards and for Ron Jones from Coventry. I was twenty-five years old, but probably just as nervous as Gareth. No, I was worse.

Nerves and what the boys in Rhigos called 'living on the edge' have always been my problem.

The return journey to Rhigos was terrible. I'd had a bit of a night out on the red wine in Paris celebrating my first cap with John Lloyd and the rest of them. The ferry to Dover was a nightmare. I don't think I have ever been so ill! It cured me of travelling to France by sea for ever.

For matches at Murrayfield and Dublin, I still wouldn't fly, and John Lloyd had to accompany me at the request of the then coach, Clive Rowlands. We went by train to Edinburgh – those trips were real 'killers'.

To get to Dublin I'd drive to Holyhead in north Wales to catch the ferry, picking up en route, the North Wales Union representative Gwyn Roblin as my 'nanny'. And of course there was the journey back from Holyhead. The players who flew were back in their beds as I was still navigating the A470 in Wales, making sure I'd be there for the Monday shift at the colliery.

I was always a nervous jerk before any game. Friends will tell you that I would find anything to fidget with in order to distract me from what was ahead – a game! It was the same for Glynneath, Neath, Wales and finally Rhigos. I couldn't count the number of times people would shout, "Come on, Dai, we'll be late!" If it hadn't been for my mother, who was constantly shouting at me, I would have been too late for everything – and probably never got a cap.

People might have thought me aloof – I don't know. I don't think I am aloof – whatever it means. I know I am shy, and I talk very little, but I couldn't wait to get onto the field – any field. Even now, I can't wait for Saturday to watch Rhigos play in the WRU division 5, south central.

I admit that I did promise Rhigos people lifts to games, and then left them behind, totally forgetting my offer because I couldn't think of anything else other than getting on the field. I remember promising lifts to the Gnoll to my big mate Ken Grindle. He was often left standing outside the New Inn pub waiting, but I had jumped in the car, driven past Ken, who was speechless, and I'd gone on to Neath without him!

I am ashamed to say that this was not a unique occurrence. How they put up with me, I will never know. Then, and even now, I have a weakness for concentrating on details and arrangements. If I have been invited to a function, I have to ring my old pal Dai Parker to check where and when.

On international mornings I would find a bookie somewhere in Dublin, London and Cardiff. Paris was useless – besides I didn't know what a bookie looked like in France, nor how it was spelt and I didn't know much about French horses either. I didn't bet; it was just a refuge.

I suffered my own sort of pre-match stress. There'd be a lot of shouting in the changing room, a lot of huffing and puffing – but not from me. I would fidget with papers, laces, read the programme, even in French – anything – because I couldn't wait to get on that field and play. It was the same everywhere.

In that first match Dai Watkins was our captain – a nice, tidy bloke, and a match winner. He proved that in both codes. He had been brought back into the Welsh side instead of a rising star called Barry John from Llanelli.

My back row partners in that first match against France were Ron Jones from Coventry and my great friend, with words for every occasion, John Taylor. John's accent was alien to us boys from the valleys, but his commitment was second to none. It didn't matter that I couldn't understand him half the time. I can remember the late Dewi Bebb – what a genuine man he was – scoring a try with a dribble to the line in that match, but alas it wasn't a good day for a young Terry Price, a most talented footballer, who missed a shed-full of kicks. He went north after that, and I think, sadly, never fully realised his potential. He is no longer with us either. But what a player! He had everything, skill, vision and power with pace.

David Nash was the coach in the earlier matches – the first ever Wales national coach. It was a huge responsibility, and yet, he was a quiet man. He was the analytical type, totally competent and supportive of all his players. I don't know why, but the team was constantly being changed by the selectors, not by Dai, and that didn't provide the cohesion that was to come in later years. Dai Nash was also the pensive type. Fine by me, but others needed a bit more passion. I am not sure how much authority he had either, or was given. The WRU committee boys spent most of their time debating rather than delivering.

A number of them didn't support having a national coach, and there was a fair amount of debate in public and in private on the merits of coaches. That hasn't changed, but the issues and personalities have – as well as the size of the contracts.

In those days, selection was a total lottery. Players were chosen who had not been seen by the 'big five' but had been written about in the *Western Mail* by J.B.G. Thomas. Caps were sometimes awarded by reputation. Mysteriously some fine players were dumped. Even Alun Pask was robbed of the captaincy, and there was a shed-full of one- or two-cap wonders floating around.

I mean no disrespect to these players, but with so much inconsistency, no plan or any direction, I thought that if they were good enough, they should have been given the opportunity to stake their claim. There were some hard characters around who I knew could do a shift for Wales, but they were never called up. Wednesday night games were full of them.

The days of the squad system were not upon us, and there were column inches in the newspapers devoted to selection and alleged club favouritism. There were popular clubs, and Neath – and a few others – was not one of them. Certainly we were not fashionable at that time according to the *Western Mail* and their correspondent. Rightly or wrongly, there was a feeling that if you played for Cardiff you were one short step from a cap.

Wales, or rather the WRU, struggled to come to terms with organisation and preparation. People were not ready to relinquish or surrender power. David Nash, unbelievably, wasn't given permission to tour with his Welsh team to Argentina. He had no authority, but the blazers did!

I can vividly recall the blazer treatment handed out to Bobby Wanbon, the number 8 from Aberavon. Gareth Edwards had already scored his first international try, and then we had a good scrum going for the England try line at Twickenham. The call had been to spread it wide so that we could win the game with a conversion under the posts. But Bobby kept it under control, and got his debut try at the back of the scrum. In marched a blazer after the game, and Bobby was told he would never play for Wales again! He didn't either – and there was a hell of a row in the changing room. We drew the match 11–11.

The blazer no doubt retired to be 'entertained' by the RFU, leaving us bewildered by the reprimand. Some things didn't change at all, for a long period.

But I was aware that there were some great young players around me, and they included Gareth and Gerald, with the experience of Bev Price and Denzil Williams.

There was one match to go in the Five Nations in my first

season, and that will only be remembered for the performance of a 19-year-old schoolboy, quiet in the changing room, who had never played full back in his life at senior level, before being selected for his country in that position.

I scored my first try for Wales, Gerald scored two, but this was Keith Jarrett's day. Just out of school, normally a centre, but picked for his country out of position at full back. If I had been the man to pick up a stray bounce in my own half, and race all the way to the line to score, and then convert my own try from the touchline, I would think myself something special. But Keith didn't, it wasn't his manner, but the inner glow must have been warm. A try, two penalties and five conversions, and England were sent packing with a 34–21 defeat. You see, they didn't play that badly – but you could not script Mr Jarrett's debut! The stuff of dreams.

Wales played their next game against New Zealand in the autumn of 1967. I wasn't picked – and John Jeffrey took my place. Wales fatally picked five new caps against Brian Lochore's New Zealand. Not only that, Brian Thomas, a lock, my rugged rascal friend from Neath, was picked as a prop, and the late Norman Gale, captain and hooker from Llanelli, took the penalty kicks! It was also the international emergence of a famous halfback partnership between Barry John and Gareth Edwards. But it wasn't going to be an easy afternoon for them either.

Preparation, by today's standards for an international, was a farce. Rhigos, my club, spend better quality time preparing for a division 5, south central game than we did for a full-blooded international then. We certainly didn't have a state-of-the-art sports centre, nor a battalion of coaches, managers, statisticians and dieticians. But then I'm not quite sure what they all do. There are still only fifteen on the field!

At the beginning we would train once or twice at either the

South Wales Police ground at Waterton Cross in Bridgend or, later, on Clive's favourite beach at Aberavon. Thousands of people would turn up to watch, which was quite clever in a way. It placed pressure on us to perform at practice. There were Sunday and Thursday sessions.

I found it quite difficult to adapt to this, since it invariably required me to change shifts, muck out the stables and sheds and tend to the animals at home before venturing down to the open sessions, with the TV cameras and press waiting. Not being the best timekeeper in the world, I often turned up with the coal dust of a shift on my eyes and face – probably stinking as well. Clive Rowlands loved that! But it was not for effect, I can assure you. Feeding the stock was more important than pleasing a blazer!

I'm not sure how the London Welsh boys managed. This was before the M4 had been completed. I can remember the mini John Dawes had, but down they came, half a dozen of them, packed like sardines in two cars – the hope of Wales! I think they must have stayed with J.P.R.'s parents in Bridgend. But I had to go back to Rhigos and tend to the animals after those training sessions. Sometimes the players stayed at Aberavon above the Afan Lido. I am reliably informed that it was not five-star quality and a last resort.

At the beginning, on home international weekends, I worked the early colliery shift on Thursday, left a bit early, and then drove down to Cardiff or Bridgend, and returned home after training. Pre-match accommodation had not been heard of in those days.

On the morning of a match in Cardiff, I'd drive down again, with Tom Tai Cwpla and Dai Pumps as passengers.

Away matches were more of a problem – lost shifts and finding someone to look after the animals. In fairness, the NCB looked after me well, since the area director Mr Phillip Weekes was a massive Welsh rugby fanatic, and friends at Rhigos were also marvellous and supportive. But the logistics were difficult.

Some of those training sessions were fierce, often more challenging than the matches. There were a few scraps I can tell you, and you'd have to watch out. They were a bit tribal as well, with the Neath boys looking after their own, and later the Pontypool front row would deal with any challengers for their Welsh positions in a very uncompromising manner. But once you were selected, that was it!

All for one – and one for all.

For some of us in the pack, stamina and strength was never reliant on gyms and weight training. Glyn Shaw and I were miners, Delme worked on pylons in west Wales, others worked in steel. Hard men in Welsh club rugby were overlooked for national selection because, quite frankly, the selectors never sought our opinions.

If they had, they would have been told about players who were quite a handful on Saturday afternoons. The success of the 1970s might have come earlier if clubs such as Aberavon, Bridgend, Ebbw Vale and Maesteg had been watched on a regular basis.

However, in retrospect there were defining moments and decisions which gave birth to one of the most successful periods in Welsh rugby.

First, Clive Rowlands was made the Welsh coach, in tandem with Ray Williams as coaching organiser. The impact of Ray Williams can never be underestimated. John Dawes emerged as an influential and inspirational quiet captain and thinker. The Australian dispensation law was introduced, which did not allow kicking to touch from outside the twenty-five-yard line. Wales travelled to New Zealand, Australia and Fiji on a suicide tour, and we were battered by the All Blacks, which prompted a major rethink. Clive persuaded Gerald during a plane journey down under that his best position would be wing, and not centre. All these were major factors and influences for the successful side of the 1970s.

A new back row was also introduced at Murrayfield in 1969, consisting of my late great friend Mervyn Davies, John Taylor and William David Morris – two former centres and one who'd had ambitions of being a professional football player. Mervyn and John were both teachers. They knew things I didn't – but not on a rugby field.

We were to play eighteen times together, with the excellent Denis Hughes of Newbridge featuring in that period as well.

John 'Bas' Taylor, was a 'flyer' and exceptionally disruptive. He could also talk, and I can remember shouting at him when Clive told him to take a line-out training session. He'd use words I was never taught in Rhigos primary. So I shouted at him that I would need a dictionary to understand what the calls were.

The three of us had words on the field as well – not that many, but if one of us missed a man, there would be a short and sharp exchange.

"He was your man, Mervyn."

"No he wasn't, Dai. First man up is yours."

"What number did he have on his back, then?"

"Eight." A sheepish answer.

"Your man then, Merv."

The exchange would continue with various expletives being exchanged, but not for long. You don't have time at that level of rugby for a mid-match conference. And anyway, I had so much respect for both of them.

From the beginning, under Clive, I was told to follow. "Follow Gareth and protect him, and then follow the ball." That was always my game plan. 'Bas' would disrupt, Mervyn would win ball or tackle, and my role was sweeper and support. I was given two nicknames 'Poacher' and 'Shadow' – the latter became the most popular. 'Bas', 'Swerve' and 'Shadow' – sounds like a cartoon series!

We were not really that organised. We certainly weren't given folders or dossiers and a library of stats. Clive would drill the forwards, and John Dawes would take the backs. We knew what our role was – to support the boys behind. We knew that we had the guile and pace behind to get us out of trouble, and the flair to attack. Clive's one-liners was the forwards' basic coaching manual. That is not to say that we forwards always played second fiddle to the glamour boys. We had our moments too.

Mervyn was an exceptional player. He could win ball in the air and on the ground. Our job as flankers was to get to the opposition and make the opposition turn inside to the awaiting Merv. It was simple and effective. Unless you were close, you would not appreciate how much punishment he suffered at the rucks. He never, ever took a backward step.

The delivery to Gareth was invariably gift-wrapped by Mervyn, so that our talents behind could express themselves. Once delivered, my duties began.

Gareth, if he saw a gap, was explosive. He had been an exceptional athlete during his schooldays under the guidance of Bill Samuel. He was also a hurdler, and more often than not the first man up, the opposition only touched his jersey, and little else. And as for determination, he could turn defences around in a second. He could spring into action like a low level missile. And part of the reason why Barry was allowed so much time was the two-man attention given by the opposition to Gareth.

He had developed a massive spin pass – more ground for me to cover – but this allowed Barry, and later Phil Bennett, time and position to look around for options. Then it was more instinct than game plan.

Gareth was also our marketing contact with Arthur Young, the Adidas rep. The first boots I ever had were bought by my mother from the Co-op in Aberdare – brown, high ankle with rubber studs.

Being part of the Welsh team was a different world. We were being offered boots and kit by Mr Young and Gareth was the negotiator. This was a problem for some of the boys, who had comfortable boots made by other manufacturers. I can still remember a few last-minute boot-painting sessions in the changing room, to make the comfy boots look like Adidas products complete with stripes. It was just like a children's nursery school with pots of paint and brushes all over the place. Sometimes our boots were taken away by Mr Young and returned with the required stripes professionally painted. What deals were made I don't know now, and I didn't then. But we were well looked after by Gareth.

I do remember Barry handing me a new pair, and telling me "Don't worry, Dai, you can pay me next week." Cheeky bugger!

Whereas we had some exceptional forwards during my playing career with Wales, we were blessed with some of the finest backs Wales has ever seen.

Much has been written about Gareth, Barry and Phil – match winners all. So too was Gerald Davies, and I would defy anyone to shadow him. That jink of his created a vacuum, and it wasn't only the opposition who would have to adjust their rugby satnavs in full flight. There was anticipation in the air whenever Gerald was given the freedom to move. I am not talking about the 60,000 crowd, I am talking about us as a back row, selected for stalking him. It was impossible! Just the finest runner I have ever played with.

It was slightly easier with John Bevan, because you knew that with his speed and immense strength exactly what he was going to do. One arm for the hand-off, the other with the ball safely placed for the inside pass. That is unless he had bulldozed his opponent into submission.

Maurice Richards was another. He was exceptionally quick and explosive, and full of determination. He was a nightmare to shadow, but a joy to watch. Maurice was born to attack.

There were those who could jink, dazzle and dance, those who could glide, but as a flanker there were two players who I appreciated much more than the headliners. John Dawes and Arthur Lewis were my sort of players. John would guide the team through the defensive and attacking phases like an orchestral conductor, and his passes would always place you in a better position. He didn't deliver bad passes. He wanted fluidity, and his pre-match approach as captain was always methodical and analytical. It was no surprise when he was asked to captain the Lions.

Ebbw Vale's Arthur Lewis was not really appreciated as he should have been. His entry into the line was always well timed, and he could bowl people over. His passing, his timing, the same as John Dawes, was superb, and the combination of the two in defence and counterattack was hugely appreciated by the back row.

And of course there was the 'Top Cat' factor – Clive Rowlands OBE, Lord of Cwmtwrch (upper and lower) and the man who didn't pass the ball out against Scotland in the infamous 111 line-out game.

I sensed an immediate rapport with Clive. He could talk from dawn to dusk about his passion for rugby and Wales. He probably talked about it in his sleep. We came from similar mining villages, same kind of people, same expectations, so he knew exactly what it meant for me to play for Wales and to represent Rhigos.

I had never come across anyone quite like him.

Half the stories he tells in rugby dinners aren't true, but he tells them with such conviction that you want them to be true. He was the same in the changing room. Clive would have you believe that there was no opposition. It was all about *our* performance.

I would hate to meet him on St David's Day, because international match days were bad enough.

There was nothing academic about Clive. It was about commitment, the jersey and Wales. Add to that your duty to perform for any relatives of yours he knew who were at the match, the thousands of Welsh supporters who had travelled to Paris, Dublin or Murrayfield and those who couldn't. What had it cost them to support us? We couldn't let them down. Clive cared about people, and he made us aware of our responsibilities.

Yes, it is quite true that during one of his evangelical pre-match changing-room rants, I had my hands over my ears, and Clive thought I was in a motivational trance. I asked him to be quiet for a minute, since I was listening to a horse race commentary from Kempton or Newmarket. It broke the ice that day, since everybody laughed. More importantly we went out and won.

The Rowlands sermons were legendary. Some players liked the Owain Glyndŵr call to arms, others didn't. Come to think of it, he would have made a formidable preacher, or a twentieth-century patron saint of Wales.

I wasn't immune to his passion, but I didn't care much for the theatrics. I was normally one of the first out of bed and into flannels and blazer. I'd be togged up before breakfast, primarily because I wanted to get out of the team hotel and find a bookie. It was a distraction, not a compulsion. After the game, a win or defeat, I'd find a corner for a chat with John Lloyd and Delme or with Tom Tai Cwpla and Dai Pumps if they were around.

Clive appreciated that I would not respond to the fire and brimstone speeches because he had the ability to gauge what made each one of us tick. His personal chats with individuals were an important part of his approach. He built up a reservoir of information about each player, and identified those who wanted to be motivated by his Agincourt speeches and those who were content with a quiet word. You shouldn't need much motivation with a red jersey on your back, and once you heard the Welsh crowd singing away before we took to the field at the Arms Park, or the National Stadium as it became, that should have sufficed. He hardly mentioned anything about your opposite numbers – he only cared about your performance. Other coaches would give you a full analysis of the opposition, and these days they have libraries of tapes and stats which would have bored me stiff!

For Clive, in the hours before kick-off, it was all about Wales and the collective will. We'd have scrummaging practices in hotel rooms and changing rooms until he was convinced that we had the right attitude. If we didn't, he would pout and walk off, but return later with a fag burning brightly. He never gave in, as he later bravely proved in his battle against cancer. In earlier days, however, especially on the touchlines, I don't know how many fags he smoked. Probably more, when we were not doing so well. The friendly Arms Park groundsman Bill Hardiman would know after a game how we had played, by counting Top Cat's fag-ends.

That hour, before going out onto the field, was the period I hated most. I would fret and fidget, open the programme but never read it. I would speak very little, since there were so many other good talkers around. I would call them the 'huffers' and 'puffers' – people who needed to be motivated by noise and shouting. Bobby Windsor, in his corner, would already have been prepared by the legendary Ray Prosser. He would attack each game as if it were a Pontypool match, and I knew from my Neath experience what that might involve. It was good to have him on my side! Bobby was a more than adequate replacement for Geoff Young.

For home matches Clive used to take us out onto the neighbouring Cardiff club ground for a few practice runs. It was a good distraction, and thoroughly enjoyed by the fans walking towards the stadium. Clive would make sure that we scored from every move in those sessions. The fans applauded, our confidence grew, and then back into the dressing room for a few last thoughts.

Mervyn, Bas and I would have a quiet last-minute chat. It was more of a ritual than anything, since we knew what we had to do.

You could hear the noise of the crowd as the minutes slowly ticked away to the anthems and kick-off. Adrenalin – Anticipation – Apprehension – Anthems. It never changed.

Gareth must have had about a dozen hamstrings for the amount of time he spent on the massage table. He treated it like his personal valet service – right up until the time to go.

Gerry Lewis, the physio, in charge of everything, kit, cinema tickets, team meetings and hamstrings would roam around like a mother hen, keeping an eye on the clock. Gerry was ever present, always with a kind or encouraging word. He was the complete opposite to me – he could keep time.

Blazers would enter to say something about luck and playing well – and then depart. I didn't have a problem with them, except when they asked "Fit?" It was a funny question to ask, as you were about to face a 50,000 crowd demanding a win against the opposition.

But these were the blazers who selected. So they had to be respected.

We went through a few captains in those early years, and each one of them had my respect, though they were entirely different. Dai Watkins and Ben Price of Newport were outstanding players and good leaders, but it wasn't until John

Dawes became skipper that I realised the demands involved. John would say little until it was appropriate for him to do so. He had a huge understanding and feel for the game, those around him, and their abilities.

The basic message was to move the ball, and with the backs we had it was a sound strategy. In the middle of our three-quarter attacks we had John and Arthur Lewis, both supreme feeders, who could give the receiver that extra yard to exploit. Rarely did they give a bad pass.

'Sid' Dawes was no Clive Rowlands – and when John became coach, those quiet reassuring and analytical moments in the changing room before a game were always precise and to the point. John would allow mistakes if you were trying something. What he would not appreciate was not trying something. Expression was everything to John, and as players we embraced that.

If there was one defining international game at the beginning of my Wales career, it was our defeat against France at the Arms Park. I'd already been exposed to Ireland's Ken Goodall, an exceptional opponent, but it was the all-conquering French team of 1968 that made an impression.

The Camberabero brothers, Guy and Lilian, were at halfback, they had Joe Maso in the middle, and in Walter Spanghero and Christian Carrère they had two of the toughest opponents I had ever met. They were simply awesome, and on that day we didn't cope, even in typical wet and windy Welsh conditions. I was a pupil in the classroom that day. I have never believed that the French always play better with the sun on their backs. I know better!

It was a benchmark moment for us. We did react, because after that French game, we didn't lose a home game for fourteen years. You were there to play, but also to learn – and we did just that. It prepared us for the toughest match I would ever play in, and that was against the same opponents – the French in 1971. More of that later, since it was such a physical battle.

I have never taken much notice of Welsh rugby politics – there's just too much of it. But during this period, it was particularly active. I'd have more success in rounding up sheep at home on my own than trying to get our union representatives to collectively agree on anything.

Within the WRU some were advocating that we had to have a coaching system at national and club level. Some disagreed, since the prospect of paying someone for his expertise didn't go down well with those who thought that they were the experts, especially the big five – the selectors. It was a row that became bitter and personal. But with the likes of Ray Williams, thankfully, common sense would prevail, but not just yet. The game had moved on, but the selectors of a different generation had not.

Wales had accepted an invitation to tour Argentina – not a full international tour, but a development tour. Dai Nash, the first national Welsh coach, was our coach at the time, but the union refused to let him travel to South America with his team. There were resignations over this issue, including Dai's, and the whole mess was cleared up when the WRU vice-president was appointed coach: a certain Mr Clive Rowlands.

It was a brutal tour. On the field the Pumas used just about every dirty trick in the book – 'boots, studs and saddles'. They didn't have to, because for a young Welsh development team, their physicality and size would have been enough.

The crowds were brutal too. We had everything chucked at us, mainly bottles. I don't know why they were so aggressive. It was a very uncomfortable feeling, and the presence of the army with guns on every street corner did nothing to placate us.

The skipper was a young emerging John Dawes, but the man who impressed the Argentinians was a 19-year-old given the nickname 'Castra' – a fortress – none other than J.P.R. Williams.

The other problem with this tour was that we were stuck in a country club, the Hurlingham, in the middle of the country. It was probably for our own security, because you could not move in Argentina without noticing the military presence. But the boys got bored – apart from J.P.R. taking on all-comers on the tennis courts, showing us why he had played at Wimbledon as a junior – and me. Why me?

There were horses galore there and gaucho cowboys – and I would drag Delme and John with me whenever I heard hooves. These were exceptional horsemen, grit hard, but also ruthless with their animals – which I didn't like. There was one experience I shall never forget – nor would the Welsh boys watching.

The horsemen were going through their routines, and one of the horses broke a leg. It was killed on the spot through the heart with a long knife, and the blood poured everywhere. It was totally ruthless. I could not believe the brutality of it, and it upset me for some considerable time. It still does, just thinking about it.

But we did have some lighter moments. Handel Rodgers was our manager, and Clive was the "unofficial coach". Both were challenged to get on the back of a horse – and in fairness they did, in their smart blazers and trousers, that is, No. 1s. I will admit now that I gave Clive's horse a good smack, and it bolted with Clive hanging on for dear life! You should have heard the screams in Welsh and the expletives! Handel didn't do too well either.

I chased on my own horse, and brought Clive's horse under control – but not Clive! He'd always claimed that Welsh was the language of heaven. On this occasion it was rather earthy.

He has always suspected that it was me who gave the

horse the smack. Now he knows, but we had a huge laugh until the next training session. I have to admit that the life of the gaucho did appeal to me. Not the brutality of it – I'd be too soft for that, but being part of that landscape, and surrounded by horses. Of that travelling party, I was probably alone in having such thoughts.

We returned to Wales. The journey from Heathrow to Wales took longer than the flight. It just showed how penny-pinching the WRU were. One bus had been booked. It left Heathrow, but all the boys had to be dropped off – on their doorsteps. So we stopped in Newport, went up the Gwent valleys, down into Cardiff, and then up the Rhondda and Cynon Valleys, and then to Swansea. I think Phil Bennett was the last to be dropped off, in Llanelli. By then, another day had passed! But at least some of those players on board had been to Rhigos!

We travelled to Murrayfield for the opening match of the next international season. The Welsh team included two new caps, both from London Welsh. One was J.P.R., and the other, Mervyn Davies. Clive was also on board as the new coach – a permanent position by now. He must have been immense in the corridors of power, exactly as he had been on the field. The team was being re-built, so too was the Arms Park.

It was a good season, since we comfortably beat Ireland, in a rather bad-tempered game, swept England aside and drew with France. So confidence was high – but not for long.

Wales had accepted an invitation to tour New Zealand, Australia and Fiji. Even on paper, the schedule looked daunting. In reality, it was diabolical. The flight down under meant stops at Tehran, New Delhi, Singapore, Sydney and a small aircraft hop from Auckland to New Plymouth to meet Taranaki. Those early Lions tours by cruise ships had it easy! And can you imagine our current squad accepting such arrangements?

It was rightly called the 'suicide tour'. And when we arrived in New Plymouth in the early hours of the morning we were asked to sing 'Calon Lân' to some elderly ladies in Welsh costumes. We were hardly West End material.

What might loosely be called the 'dirt-trackers' were selected and given a run in the first game of the tour which was a draw against Taranaki. So the rest of us watched and waited for the next game. A few days off the plane, we faced the All Blacks! That was a mistake, since we all could have benefited with a run after that back-breaking journey.

Brian Lochore as the All Blacks skipper didn't need to motivate his men. Our label as Five Nations' Champions was sufficient.

It was my first encounter against the All Blacks in a Welsh jersey, a team I much admired. I had less admiration for them when the great Colin Meads broke Jeff Young's jaw. There was some jersey pulling, but the reaction was ruthless and unwarranted. These guys were on a different playing planet. A tour by an European side to New Zealand was rare. It was much anticipated, and no All Black would want to be part of a losing side on their own soil. They had bags of attitude and determination, and we didn't do ourselves any justice at all in the first Test. Keith Jarrett missed all his kicks, five in all, and to add insult to injury, Ken Gray, one of the all-time great props, shoved J.P.R. aside for a try. Welcome to New Zealand! And we had to face them again in fourteen days. We were swept aside. 'Calon Lân?'

The 33–12 scoreline in the second Test suggests an improvement on the 19–0 drubbing in the first match. But, in all honesty, this again was a lesson from the forward masters of world rugby.

They were relentless, and any mistakes or looseness in

our play was severely punished. That pack of Meads, Gray, Lahore, Kirkpatrick, McLeod, with Sid Going snapping behind, was probably the best ever – then and now. Not even Twmws playing at prop could hold them.

True, Maurice Richards scored a wonder try for Wales with changes of pace, but in reality, the Five Nations' champions tag was long forgotten before we left New Zealand. What wasn't forgotten by the Welsh boys was the referee Pat Murphy – the man who jumped for joy when Fergie McCormick dropped a goal!

But why are the All Blacks so consistently good? Why is it that we cannot achieve that consistency? New Zealand is no bigger than Wales, has the same size population and we have the same passion for the game – or do we? But it requires more than just pride.

They are an island nation, and they measure their success against South Africa and Australia, and now Argentina, on a regular basis. I think that they largely dismiss the northern hemisphere and, judging by their record, they are justified in doing so. It might be deemed controversial, but I think our planning and development has fallen way behind and professionalism, or the embracing of it, has not helped. Does the All Black jersey mean more to a New Zealander, than wearing the red of Wales means to a Welshman? Not on the day of a match, but in our attitude, organisation and preparation for a game – the results tell us otherwise. It is something we have tried to learn from the likes of Graham Henry, Steve Hansen and Warren Gatland – all of them dyed-in-the-wool All Blacks.

I feared then that we were light years behind in development. I fear that even more now, since our current young generation have fit thumbs for playing Xboxes, but little else is fit. It starts there, with the youngsters.

The All Blacks, South Africa, Australia and France have

rules and disciplines when dealing with young players. These rules encourage participation. Their structures are also based on size, not age. We have a massive drop out of players at teenage levels. Those who remain in the game play for clubs and school teams – an inheritance of the teachers' strike, some twenty years ago. We have yet to react to this situation. Those who have left will never return, those who have stayed are playing too much and not training enough. It is a great pity that we did not respond to this at the time – even worse is the fact that we have done little since, and the competition for a child's attention to sport is far more severe, subtle and sophisticated now.

We rely on four regional teams at senior level, whereas there were sixteen first-class clubs around the time I was playing. That meant that more players were exposed to the demands of first-class competitive rugby. There were more opportunities. We now have internationals sitting on the bench in regional rugby. How *twp* is that?

The senior professional set-up puzzles me as well. I never understood why the 'valleys' were denied a team. The 'Dragons' mean little to Pontypool, Cross Keys, Newbridge and Ebbw Vale. Why should they? The Ospreys have nothing to do with Neath or vice versa. Llanelli have embraced the concept, but initially imported players from outside in key positions. The Blues went to play in the Cardiff City Stadium with the die-hard 6,000 supporters lost in a 25,000-seater stadium, but have now wisely returned. Their prominent players in recent times, however, have been Rush, Tito and Blair. What on earth have we gained?

And then to complete the picture of disharmony, we have 'proud' Pontypool recently locked in a legal battle with the WRU. Whatever the rights or wrongs in this expensive High Court case, what are we doing to ourselves in pursuit of Welsh rugby excellence? I don't pretend to understand the complexities, but what I do understand is the remit of the WRU to encourage and foster the game in Wales. Has this been accomplished by having a day or two in court, with costs of £400,000 plus, against a club with an enormous contribution to Welsh rugby?

There are some exceptional players in the current Welsh set-up, and the success that they have achieved is well deserved. But, below the elite regional level, or Wales Rugby Ltd., I genuinely believe that we could be in trouble before long. We have too many struggling clubs, too many 14- and 15-year-old youngsters drifting off, and far too many 'old hand international mercenaries' at the senior level drifting in, and some of our best players drifting out.

Most of the best All Blacks have come from farming stock – people possibly like me, who used strength on a daily basis. True, there would have been fewer distractions for the New Zealand youngsters in those days, but with the world getting smaller due to communication, they still produce the best. How? If I knew, I'd bottle it and take it back to Rhigos. What I do know is that 'hardness' is not born in a gym.

It is no freak occurrence that currently one of our most outstanding forwards in Wales is Dan Lydiate – a farmer from mid Wales. There is no substitution for innate strength.

During my playing days there was the realisation that we could not compete with the robust drive of the New Zealand forwards. There was little point in taking them on at their own game. We could, however, counter with our backs, and angles of running. New Zealand back play was methodical and pretty predictable. Ours was not, especially with the likes of Gareth, Barry, Benny, Gerald and Maurice. All had flair, and this generation was to give birth to the 'Welsh way' of rugby.

At least there was some fun and relaxation on this desperate and ill-conceived tour of down under. We were invited by

'Tiny' White, a legendary and great All Black to spend some time on the coast.

Tiny had a massive yacht, and we were all placed in rubber dinghies and told to paddle out. This nearly became a major tragedy. A fair amount of beer had been drunk, and there was a great deal of mischief, notably engineered by Norman Gale and Denzil Williams. Some of the dinghies overturned, and to this day I think Dennis Hughes was lucky to survive. He was under a capsized dinghy, but somehow we managed to get him on board the yacht.

Battered and bruised, there was another plane journey for the man who hated flying! Off we went to Australia. There wasn't much *hwyl* on board!

It was on this flight that Clive Rowlands called on all his emotive persuasive powers to convince Gerald that he was a first-class centre, but probably a *world-class* wing. I am not sure whether Gerald agreed, but Clive, as ever, had his way.

'Top Cat' would have found it hard not to smile as Gerald scored one of his scintillating tries in the next match against Australia from his new position. What a player he was – one of the best ever. And humble too.

We defeated Australia – just! It mattered little, since we all knew what we would have to do if we were ever to beat those All Blacks. Even scoring a try against the Wallabies could not erase those All Blacks in the land of the white cloud.

A stop off in Fiji and its beaches, strange drinks, and a 31–11 win restored the spirits. Frogs invaded our training pitch. I never knew that there were so many frogs in the world. We were serenaded with garlands of flowers, and the sight of Brian Thomas in a grass skirt and sarong, and throwing our management team, including blazers, into the hotel swimming pool did a lot to raise moral. A win against the Fijians also helped.

Yet, that was achieved in one of the hardest tackling

matches I had encountered. The Fijians simply flew and leaped into their tackles – and they were not small men either. I came off fairly bruised from that match from a number of mid-air collisions.

But, despite the laughter and the prospect of returning home, the tour had unsettled and rattled a number of the players – especially the forwards. Perhaps it had been one journey too many for some. Perhaps they knew that the benchmark set by the All Blacks was too high. It wasn't long before a few departed to rugby league; some like Ben Price, a major stalwart, retired; and a few drifted back to club rugby.

I had been around the world, but then returned to my real world of Rhigos and Tower Colliery.

A few of us were determined that we would never again capitulate as we had done in New Zealand. The tour was the birth of the successful 1970s team.

After the embarrassment of the All Black defeats, we went undefeated in thirteen games. And who should bring that run to a halt? New Zealand of course! Don't remind my good mate Glyn Shaw of that. It was his first cap!

It was an honour to play with the new generation of players and to be a part of something special. You could put up with the cold and windy beach sessions at Aberavon, because there was a game to be played, and Wales to represent. There was a common goal to express ourselves, and to establish ourselves. We'd been taught a lesson down under. Those who knew, or wanted to know, realised what had to be done.

We had to be built again and establish a style to match our talents. Our next opponents at the Arms Park in 1970 were South Africa. It was, of course, a highly controversial tour, with anti-apartheid protesters very much in evidence. Also apparent was the Welsh rain. Gareth took over the captaincy. He also took over the kicking duties. I don't know why he did that, with Barry available. Benny, also a main kicker at

Llanelli, played on the wing in that 6–6 game. Gareth scored an immense try but, alas, he missed what would have been the winning conversion.

This was a rebuilding era, after the New Zealand tour debacle, and there were quite a few interesting selections in the pipeline. Laurie Daniel from Pontypool played in one game, scored a try and kicked a conversion – but was never selected again.

The same happened to Ray 'Chico' Hopkins, that great character from Maesteg. In any other era, Chico would have won a shop-full of caps. Mind you, he would probably have sold them at a marketable rate! He was an immense and likeable character. At least he played in a winning side against the All Blacks in that famous 9–3 result at Llanelli. Something I never achieved. He also went on a Lions tour – again, something I didn't do.

He also won a match for Wales – almost on his own – against England at Twickenham, after Gareth had limped off injured. But Chico, who warmed the bench for countless games, certainly didn't warm to the idea of being the perennial sub. He is still seething and grumbling, forty or so years later, about what might have been. He finally went to rugby league, but it didn't quite work out for him. It is always a joy to see and hear him at various functions, but don't mention Gareth Edwards!

Few who were at Murrayfield for the John Taylor winning kick from the touchline will ever forget that epic encounter Wales won by a single point 18–19. Most of the boys couldn't bear to look. From Delme's palm down to Gerald's try in the corner – it was a sensational finish. The try is a repeated television archive, but how many can name the one back who did not handle in that movement. It's a favourite quiz question. It was Ian Hall, a fine robust, no-nonsense centre from Aberavon.

It was a good season, and quite rightly most of the Welsh boys were rewarded by being selected for the Lions 1971 tour to New Zealand. I wasn't. There are countless theories about the decision not to include me. I have left my thoughts on that to the back pages of this book. I'd rather concentrate on what I did with Wales and Rhigos. What I do know is that the success of the Lions was based on the Welsh experience in 1969 – and I was part of that.

It was a confidence and belief that Wales could score more tries than the opposition. Some of the scores were remarkable. Gareth had one against France, as he raced in to support J.P.R. who had himself already covered more than half the field. Then, later there was Gareth's much watched try from a scrum in the Arms Park mud. Pick up, a handoff, a kick and a hack, and a final slithering dive for the corner. Some of the skills displayed during his reign were sublime, and I will dwell on these later.

There is one other abiding memory. It was that match against the French in 1971 at Stade Colombes, where we were going for the Grand Slam.

Captained by Christian Carrère, and partnered by Benoît Dauga and Jean Paul Biermouret in the back row, with Claude and Walter Spanghero as locks, they came at us with everything they had. You could not relax for a minute because behind the scrum were the exceptional attackers Cantoni and Bertranne, and lurking behind them was the extraordinarily talented Villepreux.

As a back row we knew that we had to get amongst them with first-time tackles from the word go. But they were relentless, coming at us with power and determination. We struggled to cope with them, but cope we did. This team had developed since that embarrassing defeat against the All Blacks in 1968. Denzil Williams was a seasoned campaigner, winning his thirty-sixth cap. Alongside him was tough as teak

Jeff Young, with the young converted prop Barry Llewellyn. They never gave ground.

That match is still vivid in my mind, because it was the fastest test of my career. Every tackle had to count. The French spun the ball wide whenever they could, which meant more yards to cover.

Of course, it will always be remembered for the explosive finishing talent of Gareth Edwards, taking a scoring pass from J.P.R. who had intercepted a French attack on our own line. It will also be remembered for Barry John's nose-breaking tackle on Dauga and the felling of Montois, a man twice his size, and the ultimate gliding try with a change of direction that was then the hallmark of the Cefneithin genius. We won the game 9–5, and with it the Grand Slam. It was all over in a flash, it had been so fast. Recovery would take longer. That victory was the most satisfying of all, since our defensive qualities had matched our attacking abilities.

And though some 'royal' Cefneithin blood had been spilled on the fields of France, the whole of Wales smiled.

It was more of a club team than an international side. We went through that season largely unchanged, and the quiet technical guidance of John Dawes as skipper was a massive influence. He left the emotional stuff to Clive, but like an orchestral conductor, his role was to support talent, method and flair. It helped to have in J.P.R., John Bevan, Gerald, Arthur Lewis and the Edwards/John duet, a fantastic ensemble of gifted players. It was a pleasure to shadow them.

Most were selected for the British Lions. Barry Llewellyn and Jeff Young were not available, and Denzil and I were not selected. John Dawes was selected to skipper the Lions. Throughout his captaincy of Wales, he never lost to England.

On his triumphant return from defeating the All Blacks,

The amazing 'Invincibles' of Glynneath RFC 1961–62. I'm in the back row, third from the left

After leaving Glynneath in 1963 I joined Neath under the captaincy of Morlais Williams

(courtesy of H.G. Lewis)

The match programme for my very last game for Neath in 1975, ironically against the first senior club I represented – Penarth RFC

Neath – winners the Welsh Cup under Martyn Davies, with Dai Parker in the middle of it!
(courtesy of *South Wales Evening Post*)

Standing room only – a typical Neath vs Aberavon 'bruiser'

Neath 1971 WRU Cup winners

Proud moment – my first Welsh cap in 1967

The Welsh team in Paris – and I'm there after a ferry crossing

In action during the match at Stade Colombes
(courtesy of Miroir-Spirit, Paris)

Gareth's first game as captain, against Scotland – he's only 20 – with Gerald
looking 'mean'!

Neath's pampas boys on tour in Argentina in 1968: Glen Ball, Walter Williams, H.G. Lewis – our photographer and me
(courtesy of Jim Giddings)

The Welsh squad in Argentina, with Clive Rowlands at the helm. Most of the boys were bored stiff!
(courtesy of Jim Giddings)

The boys at the Hurlingham Club in Argentina. Back row: Brian Rees, John Jeffrey, Billy Mainwaring, Lyn Baxter, Max Wiltshire, Walter Williams, Terry Evans, Alan John. Middle Row: Andy Morgan, Glyn Turner, Bob Phillips, J.P.R. Williams, B. Butier, Tony Gray, W.D. Morris, John Lloyd, Glen Ball, S. Ferguson, Phil Bennett. Seated: Laurie Daniel, Clive Rowlands, Denis Hughes, George Morgan, John Dawes, Harry Bowcott, Norman Gale
(courtesy of H.G. Lewis)

Some of the hardest competitors ever – the Fijians – massive men

(courtesy of Caines Jannif Ltd., Suva)

Dai Parker, 'the little one', held aloft after winning the Snelling Sevens competition in Cardiff

Dai Parker with the silverware again. Member of our Tower Colliery sevens team, without having been down a mine!

One of many Welsh charity matches – with all expenses checked by the WRU (courtesy of Llwyn White)

Relaxing with my mates Denis Hughes and John Lloyd at the Bermuda Classics

Rhigos R.F.C.

||||

OFFICERS :

President : C. J. LEWIS, Esq.

Chairman : A. DAVIES, Esq.

Secretary : G. LEWIS, Esq.,
4a, Heol-y-Graig, Rhigos, Aberdare,
Mid-Glam. CF44 9YY.
Tel. : Hirwaun 811952

Treasurer : A. HAMER, Esq.

Fixture Secretary : G. THOMAS, Esq.,
24 Heol Gwangfryn, Rhigos, Aberdare,
Mid-Glam. CF44 9EJ.

Captain : CLIVE HARRIS

Vice-Captain : MIKE HARRIS

RHIGOS R.F.C

v.

A WELSH INVITATION XV

To celebrate
The Official Opening
of Rhigos R.F.C. Clubhouse

MONDAY, 11th SEPTEMBER, 1978
KICK-OFF — 6.30 p.m.
HEOL ESGYN PLAYING FIELD, RHIGOS

★

ADMISSION BY PROGRAMME

Price—25p

George Selwyn Limited, Printers, Hirwaun Industrial Estate, Aberdare. Tel. 811364

Our first fixture list as Rhigos RFC in 1977

The 'grand' announcement... Rhigos RFC clubhouse is opened in 1978!

One of my finest hours, the opening of the Rhigos clubhouse by the Lord of Upper and Lower Cwmtwrch, Clive Rowlands

The very first Rhigos team, playing at Glynneath Welfare

My workplace – Tower Colliery – with one of our resident sheep in the background

Scrubbed up for a garden party at Buck House with Delme and Bethan Thomas, Marlene and myself

Collier, horse owner, rugby player and sheep shearer!

I have done a fair bit for various charities – and some of them were plain daft! This for kidney research

We've put on weight, we've gone grey, and I barely recognised some of them. They probably didn't recognise me either! A garden party for ex-internationals at the Millennium Stadium. Where am I? In the back row of course

My first venture into the horse racing world with Princess Glory. Unfortunately there was not much glory
(courtesy of Peter Knowles)

At my Rhigos stables, chasing what, I don't know!
(courtesy of Peter Knowles)

Better fortune with Helen's Vision. She ran in Dai Walters' colours at Stratford. A great family outing

Helen's Vision in my red and black colours at Newbury, with jockey Liam Treadwell on board
(courtesy of Ian Headington)

You meet some tough boys on the reception circuits. This is Eddie Avoth, British and Commonwealth Light Heavyweight Boxing Champion. He became an actor – but so did I!

Glynneath's finest ambassador and one of my greatest friends, Max Boyce

Our 'remote' wedding on the Brecon Beacons. Marlene, my bride, Pauline and Ann, the bridesmaids and Dai Davies, my best man. And Neath were playing Ebbw Vale that afternoon!

The family – me, Marlene, Helen and Greg

My grandson,
Joseph Parry

My two grandsons
Joseph and Ben with
a Grogg of me!

he retired from playing, only to return as Welsh coach in 1974.

My mate John Lloyd took over the Welsh captaincy in 1972. 'Mr Greedy', as John was called in the Welsh camp, was another precise tactical practitioner. And could he eat! John was known to order a full breakfast to his room, and then join the others for a team breakfast as well – until he was found out. He was one of the few players who enjoyed the tour to Argentina because he must have devoured a herd of steaks! But he was a great companion, good company, no fuss and certainly one to shun the limelight. It was a good but unusual season with three wins, one postponed match because of the Irish troubles, and Barry John's retirement.

The decision not to play Ireland probably lost us back-to-back Grand Slams.

I wasn't the only one bewildered by Barry's decision. He was one of the most deceptive of all outside halves. I had a good view of those gliding runs, with ball in two hands, making opponents think and then sending them the wrong way. He was essentially quite shy, and all the adulation after the 1971 Lions tour presented problems. I did feel for him, as someone who is known to be shy, but he did have a jovial and mischievous streak in him. Barry always played with a confident smile.

It is strange that two boys from the same village – Cefneithin – Carwyn and Barry, were the architects on that winning Lions 1971 tour. Barry kicked 180 points in New Zealand but didn't reach a hundred for Wales in the Five Nations.

Barry didn't like the post-tour adulation, and Carwyn, who coached me for the West Wales side against New Zealand, was also uncomfortable with the limelight. Yet, both of them strangely chose journalism and broadcasting after packing in the game.

Carwyn was an academic, a scholarly man, a former

teacher at that great rugby school, Llandovery College. Carwyn's approach was to have a great influence on those who listened. John Dawes was one. The WRU didn't. He was given control of the Lions in 1971 by Doug Smith, and they won.

Carwyn should have been given the role of Welsh team coach. He had the respect of the players, and that goes a long, long way. But he wanted too much control over team matters, according to the union. So, knowing full well what the reaction might be, he gave them a written 'take it or leave it' offer.

Just imagine Graham Henry, Warren Gatland or Andy Robinson not being allowed control over team matters. It just shows what a visionary Carwyn was, and how blind others were. Right man – wrong time.

I am not sure who was the most fervent smoker though – Rowlands or James!

Barry decided to go, but not before he and Carwyn had organised an exceptional event. I nearly missed Barry's farewell match in Cardiff. It was an Urdd jubilee celebration game between a Carwyn James XV (1971 Lions team) and Barry's team (the Welsh Five Nations champions). The crowd was huge, almost a full house at the National Stadium and again I was a bit late leaving Rhigos. How many times have I said that? I was driving with Tom Tai Cwpla on board, but we were nowhere near the stadium for the three o'clock kick-off. I made a run for it, leaving Tom stranded in a traffic jam.

Fortunately, the game was held up because there were so many latecomers – including me. It kicked off twenty-five minutes late, and I just about made it.

To this day, my Rhigos mate Ken Grindle swears that they held up the game for me. I don't think so somehow. I agree with one of his comments, that I have been one of the most disorganised people on the planet. But it was also true that

Dai Duckham and John Spencer, stuck on a train, were also late, and there was genuine pandemonium in the changing room due to the shortage of players.

Eventually, we took to the field, to say farewell to Barry and to raise money for the Urdd.

Ken, incidentally, was disgusted with me on one quite boozy New Year's Eve, when all of us had far too much to drink, including the wives. Ken demanded that I get all my old jerseys from the attic. Our attic has rarely been visited. I don't really know what is up there except a lifetime of things having been put away. Anyway, my jerseys – Wales, Centenary, County, Neath – were all in a black plastic rubbish bag. He was outraged, but it still didn't stop him dancing around Rhigos at 4.00 a.m. in the morning in a rainbow of colours. He chose the Glamorgan County jersey, since he had represented them.

Ken took the jerseys away, washed and ironed them (or his wife did), and they are now on display at the Rhigos Club. One day I will clear out the attic. Sorry, Marlene will clean out the attic, because I hate chucking things away. I don't know where my old programmes are or some of the press cuttings I might have kept. I brought a gaucho saddle back from Argentina for Greg. That might be up there as well.

With Barry gone, in stepped Phil Bennett, who'd already been used as a utility back. But now he was ready to step into his familiar number 10 jersey. The one he wore when Llanelli beat the All Blacks 9–3!

They were two very different players. It was a darned sight harder following Phil around. Barry would glide, Phil would jink. Both were exceptional talents. One was an extrovert, the other an introvert. It didn't matter. I didn't have a clue what either would do next on the field.

I wasn't to know it at the time, but our next match gave Wales and me the best opportunity of beating the All Blacks.

The game will be remembered for a post-match incident between a security guard and the New Zealand prop Keith Murdoch.

It was also the closest we came to beating the All Blacks, as the 19–16 scoreline suggests. This was no humiliation or a repeat of the disaster down under in 1969. Delme, victorious over the All Blacks at Stradey Park, was selected as captain of Wales.

It was also a first cap for my working and Neath colleague Glyn Shaw. He was immensely strong, and physically challenging. I knew that from the daily lifting challenges at the colliery. We would also share lifts, not only to the Gnoll, but also to Cardiff. That proved to be of questionable benefit, since both of us were fairly adventurous drivers. Glyn only knew one way forward – a straight line. He drove like that sometimes as well, and there are quite a few bends between Rhigos and the Gnoll.

Few opposition props could handle Glyn. He was ruthless, and became a rugby league target from the word go.

We had our opportunities in the All Blacks match, but a few decisions didn't go our way, and a few kicks were missed. As ever, the Blacks were clinical. Murdoch disappeared after his fracas with a security guard and turned up much later in the Australian outback.

We have yet to beat the All Blacks in modern times. That hurts.

We didn't exactly set the world alight in what was to be my final season for Wales. A tour of Canada allowed a few more players to stake their claims. Gareth captained the touring party, and we overwhelmed the Canadian national team 58–20.

The scenery was exceptional, and the company jovial. It wasn't an intense tour though. So wherever we went I sought out the stables of the local Canadian mounted police, to inspect their horses. Delme and John came along with me for company, and I have to admit that this was the pinnacle of the journey for me. At least in the two Welsh tours I was selected – Argentina and Canada – I had been able to indulge in my equine passion.

I don't mean to be ungrateful to exemplary hosts. It is not in my nature. I have always appreciated hospitality wherever I have been – Cimla or Canada. The Canada tour lacked intensity – it wasn't New Zealand, Australia or South Africa. The belting that Wales had suffered in New Zealand was still a mental sore. But rock the Rockies we did!

It does make me wonder about who schedules these tours, and whether some international teams would benefit more by coming here rather than us going there. True, there are major financial and complicated considerations, and the recently established unions have to make money. But I remember talking to the Neath boys, who, much later, under Ron Waldron, travelled to Namibia under the captaincy of Neath's Gareth Llewellyn. They stayed in Windhoek for two weeks, same hotel, same faces – a place, which I was told, resembled Pontypridd on a bad Saturday night – and yet they were expected to turn in international performances.

Will the power base of international rugby ever change? I wish it would.

Eddie Butler's Wales were defeated by Romania in Bucharest, and Wales were defeated by Western Samoa in the 1999 World Cup – but it is still a fairly elite and exclusive international rugby club as far as resources are concerned. I travel a lot supporting Rhigos these days, and our resources are lacking as well. And we are not alone.

There has always been a class distinction in rugby. It is also true of development as well. Since the professional era came about, the gap between the 'haves' and 'have nots' has widened. A talented player from Samoa, Fiji, Romania,

Argentina or Canada is more likely to be found playing in France, Italy or the UK. What does that do for their game development back home?

I understand the pressure on rugby administrators when the game went professional. If it hadn't, there were people like Kerry Packer and Rupert Murdoch waiting in the wings, with every intention of hijacking the game. We in Wales were constantly losing quality players to rugby league. Something had to give, and once that decision was made to pay players – that is where a massive division was created.

In Wales we have struggled with the professional game, because we are too small a nation to sustain it. The introduction of a salary cap for our regions was inevitable, but that has only signalled a player exodus. In recent months, hardly a day goes by when one of our senior squad follows the dollar and decides to play outside the Welsh regions. I can't blame them.

The regions themselves are struggling, and out of town Legoland stadiums rarely entice capacity crowds. Call me a dinosaur, but you couldn't match the buzz of a full Gnoll, Stradey Park or Sardis Road. They were magic grounds. We had tight-knit rugby communities which have now been replaced by nonsensical territories or regions.

Yet the blazers still go on their trips, hold their conferences and issue edicts. The top boys running the game earn massive salaries, whereas we scratch for an income to keep the game going! The buses from Rhigos are £400 a trip! The salaries played to leading players would balance the books in many a Welsh rugby club. And how many of our regions are 'in the black'?

I just don't understand it. Nor do I understand people paying £77 for an international ticket, when the ball is barely in play for twenty minutes. If you attend every single game, now that the southern hemisphere sides are annual visitors, it costs a small fortune, especially if you support your regional side as well. Let's put it into context. To watch the Welsh team of the 1970s play at Twickenham some of the stand seats in the lower sections cost only £1 10 /–. OK, salaries and everything else have gone up, but have the powers taken into account that regular top-class rugby is well beyond the reach of many pockets.

The game itself is now about retention rather than exploitation. Commentators will point out the number of possession phases a team has accomplished before releasing the ball to an overcrowded and zoned defensive wall. We wait, impatiently, for a phase of broken play, because that is now the most productive area of attack. Ask Shane Williams, George North or Alex Cuthbert.

I will probably get in trouble for saying that. But I don't think I am alone in thinking it. I hear the same things said in Rhigos, Glynneath, Cwmgwrach and every Neath old players' function.

That old players' function is held annually in the Glyn Clydach Hotel, just outside Neath. It is a great opportunity to meet old friends, and a few foes. It is about memories. Yet, most of those attending would have had a full life outside rugby during their playing days. The game was a pastime, even though it was demanding. I am not sure whether I would have coped with a nine to five rugby job, reporting to and staying at the WRU Vale of Glamorgan, or Llandarcy training centre on a weekly basis. Would I have been any fitter? I know that I would not have coped in terms of size. W.D. Morris back row 6', 13 st. George North, current Welsh wing, 6' 5", 16 st. 5 lb. Frightening!

It is, of course, a totally different game these days, and the modern players are under constant media scrutiny. It was this intrusion that probably caused Barry John to quit when he did. But some of them thrive on it. I just can't see some of our boys signing up for *Strictly Come Dancing* somehow.

My last season in a Welsh jersey was a disappointment. It also heralded the beginning of the Pontypool invasion. Under the no-nonsense coach and former Wales and British Lion Ray Prosser, Pontypool were beginning to develop a forward unit that was to become a dominant force in Welsh rugby. Prosser was coach to Pontypool for eighteen years, and he had played in a winning Lions team against the All Blacks. I envy him that.

His influence on Welsh forward play, based on fitness, hard work and a fair bit of intimidation cannot be underestimated. No team fancied a Wednesday night trip to the 'Pooler' in years to come. Price, Windsor, Faulkner, Perkins, Staff Jones, Huish, Butler, Cobner, Squires – a formidable unit, and the rumour was that Lord Lucan played outside half since the ball was hardly surrendered to the backs. I have often thought that match between the Neath team of the 1970s and the Pontypool team of the 1980s would have filled the Arms Park. Frank Warren could have been involved in promoting that one. Bobby Windsor was the first Pooler man to emerge, quickly followed by Terry Cobner. Alan 'Panther' Martin, one of the great Welsh servants from Aberavon, came into the side as well.

Our opponents in November 1973 were Australia. They were nowhere as powerful as they had been, or were to become. I scored a try, so too did Bobby and Gerald and we won comfortably, 24–0.

Terry Cobner won his first cap as a 28-year-old, a year older than Barry John, who had retired. It was then the start of the Five Nations campaign, a season where we struggled to gain consistent momentum. I don't know why, but during that season there were a fair amount of significant changes, especially in the backs. 'Cobs' scored a try on his debut against Scotland, but it was a pretty dour affair. Ireland missed their kicks, nine in all, in a drab drawn Dublin match, and we drew with the French in Cardiff as well. Hardly headline stuff!

We headed for Twickenham, hoping for some salvation. It was not to be. J.P.R. was missing, Delme was brought out of retirement, and we were denied a perfectly good try by the referee John West. Not only that, the RFU had decided not to play 'Hen Wlad Fy Nhadau' at the beginning of the game. Max, down the road at Glynneath, was incensed but motivated to write a few jibes about "blind Irish referees". It went down well in Rhigos, I can tell you – probably further afield as well!

It was a very disappointing 16–12 defeat.

It was Clive's last game as coach – and a defeat to England did not go down well at all in Cwmtwrch. Defeat was never acceptable to Clive, but defeat to England was a national disaster. People might recall Clive's response to a journalist's question at the 1987 Rugby World Cup after Wales had been hammered by the All Blacks.

"Where does this leave Welsh rugby?" was the question.

"We go back to beating England every year," was the Rowlands retort. It was not to be, in his last game in charge.

Clive's departure signalled the arrival of John Dawes as Welsh coach, and also heralded a major rebuilding programme. I knew Wales would be in good hands, since John, though totally different to Clive in his approach, was superbly analytical. He was always supportive of the players who tried to express themselves on the field. He never criticised the player who would try to invent opportunities. He would if you didn't. I liked his approach as captain, and I knew he would make a fine coach.

It was significant that the British Lions 1974 party selected to go to South Africa under Willie John McBride featured only two Welsh forwards, but six Welsh backs. Wales had a poor season, but worse was to follow, for me personally.

Neath had an end-of-season game against Llanelli, which was always a blustering and competitive encounter. I always enjoyed playing against Llanelli. They were combative and full of talent. But so were we.

I was caught in a tackle by my fellow international Tommy David. I was spun around, and heard my leg crack. I had broken my cruciate ligaments. I knew it was serious. The pain was unbelievable. But I refused to go to hospital. I can't stand hospitals.

It was to be the end of my first-class career. You could not imagine the pain of that tackle. But I think I already knew I would not walk the tall walk again. Others had views on Tommy's tackle and expressed them. I thought a few weeks off might do the trick, and it did get better.

Normally when hurt, I wouldn't show it. I thought it was a sign of weakness if you had to draw attention to yourself. I was always loathe to call a trainer onto the field. But this injury was different.

7

Mining and Media

I WAS NEVER comfortable being in the spotlight. I found the whole experience overwhelming. If I saw a television crew, I'd avoid them. There are those who are comfortable with focus and attention – good luck to them. I am not one of them.

On the morning of one of those training sessions at Waterton Cross in Bridgend, I would be down the pit at Tower with my mates doing some manual work, some of them effing and blinding, talking about pints, their wives and their women and then, suddenly, within a few hours, I'd find myself in front of television cameras and press photographers – let alone hundreds of supporters.

I am sure that my kind of mental 'down the pit and onto the field' preparation would be frowned upon now, but I had little choice. Focused? I'd have a quick pithead shower, put on a tracksuit (if I'd remembered to pack one), and jump in the car. Then it was time to enter into a different shift and another world. And this one was unreal!

The boys who play for Wales now have agents, are given media briefings and some are selected for press conferences. I don't envy them being confined in the spacious Vale of Glamorgan headquarters, but I do feel some of them need a life beyond rugby and training. How are they going to cope with reality?

I suspect that a few of the current players who have got

into trouble in late-night incidents have been letting off steam, because they are so bored with the cloistered routine.

We've had to embrace professionalism almost overnight. With it, rugby has had to change. For over a hundred years Welsh rugby was amateur, but in twelve months it had to become professional. It was absurd. How could well-meaning committee men in clubs, working for a living, cope with it? It was too sudden, chaotic and ill planned.

That decision in a South African hotel, and then endorsed in what they called the Paris Accord was, in terms of rugby in Wales, the most damaging development ever. Our game was dragged into a professional era... Cardiff, Swansea, Rhigos, Blaina, Bethesda, Cwmtwrch et al... We were not ready for it...

As for the laws of the game, it beggars belief. For a game that wants to expand throughout the four corners of the globe it is now, with the rare exception, a game for big physical specimens. Don't get me wrong. When I see the likes of Jamie Roberts, Jonathan Davies, George North and Alex Cuthbert punch holes in oppositions' defences, I am the first out of the chair.

Yet, in a small village you will not have the luxury of 6' 5", 16 st. physical blokes playing the same laws that demand that. My friend Max Boyce sang a song about the Welsh 'outside half factory' where the likes of Dai Watkins, Barry John, Phil Bennett, Jonathan Davies, Dai Richards, Malcolm Dacey were coming off the conveyor belt – all match winners. What place is there for such players in the modern game? Few of them were picked for their tackling abilities, but now they are. They were picked for their brilliance at being inventive, incisive and for their natural match-winning capabilities.

Behind the ten-yard line, all the outside half has to do is kick for territory and hope for a period of broken play. Dull!

Today's player is an extremely fit physical specimen, and

they need to be, since the game is all about physical crash ball retention. You are now there to take a man out, not floor him with a tackle. It is like American football without the helmets and padding.

And we, too, at Rhigos, as the laws dictate, have to play the same game! I do worry about the injury rate, and I suspect that many of our contemporary players will suffer in later years. My generation did, and I am suffering with aches and pains now. But I think that the modern players will be confronted by arthritic joints much earlier in life. The sad irony is that they might well live longer in pain than my generation.

Some of our lot, and I know comparisons are futile, had nine-to-five jobs, responsibilities beyond the game, and for me, the game was the place to let off steam. It was also welcome escapism.

Our day-to-day jobs also gave us a diversion from rugby, or was it the other way around? Some were teachers, others steelworkers, farmers or reps. You might have been in the spotlight on Saturdays and Wednesday nights, but you were breadwinners for the rest of the time – and that was a priority, for them, their wives and family.

I worked at Tower Colliery for twenty years, getting there by six o'clock every morning for an eight-hour shift. Before that I worked at the Pandy Colliery, and the drift mine in Rhigos as a blacksmith striker. My job whilst playing for Wales at Tower was mainly keeping supplies available to the boys underground, and naturally that involved a great deal of lifting, heaving and dragging. There were trapdoors and cages to navigate, and the men underground would soon tell you if you weren't up to it with rings, coils or timber – Welsh cap or not. But the camaraderie was fantastic, and it still is, since we have an annual reunion every year, though the numbers, sadly, are getting fewer every year. The coalfields were struck off, and now the boys are dying.

I thoroughly enjoyed it all, and it was a sad day when Mrs Thatcher dangled redundancy payments before the men when mine closures were introduced. Tyrone O'Sullivan, our union rep, did his best to keep Tower open from his little cubicle, but many of the men didn't qualify for the large handouts and became disillusioned.

It is difficult to comprehend that in my lifetime the whole of south Wales has been transformed. Whole communities have disappeared, the slag heaps have either been removed or are now green. There are fewer jobs around, and if you want work, you have to be prepared to move or travel.

My son Greg travels from Rhigos to the Midlands every day to his work place. What does the future hold for his children and my grandchildren?

I also have difficulty in comprehending that some of the largest salaries in Wales are being paid to rugby players. The modern-day players are rewarded with incredible weekly pay packets, not on the same scale as the obscene amounts given to football players, but I have often wondered what our lot would have been worth. What price for Gareth, Barry, Phil or Gerald? And it does worry me whether we in Wales can actually afford professional rugby. What is the point of having half-empty, state-of-the-art stadiums? Call me old-fashioned and stubborn, but give me a packed Gnoll, Stradey Park or St Helens every time. I doubt whether the affinity we had with our supporters is there today. You'd be told on Monday at the colliery how well you'd played on Saturday. You wouldn't have to buy the *Western Mail* or be scrutinised by action replays.

As far as the media was concerned, there were quite a few of our squad who didn't require tuition in communication skills. Gareth, Barry, Brian Price and Gerald had no problems with the cameras, and Clive Rowlands was a natural. Others, the quiet ones, like me, John Lloyd, Delme Thomas, the Pontypool boys, would tolerate the media presence, because it was part of the scene. Rarely did we get involved, though later, John, as captain and coach was thrust into the limelight. But as a teacher, he was well equipped to handle anything.

I was told to avoid certain reporters by players who were in the know. But then I don't think I gave many interviews, if any at all, and I think the media boys quickly found out that I didn't have much to say anyway.

I would watch the evening news, and sometimes see me running and training on the field, but that was it. Naturally, back at Tower, the boys would give me a ribbing, especially after an international. You can't hide underground, and both Glyn Shaw and I took a fair amount of good-natured leg-pulling. One thing, for certain, they were all supporters. And they were proud of us. If they thought you'd had a bad game, or a bad result, you would know. They wouldn't talk at all.

It helped to have people like Gareth, Phil and Clive around. Clive especially, played for Wales and talked for Wales – in both Welsh and English, and his passion has never subsided.

I didn't get selected for talking, that wasn't part of my job description. I still find it difficult when asked to say something at a function. I think I've got a little better at it, but not much. I was pretty speechless at my seventieth birthday party at the Rhigos Club. The audience was full of my mates from Wales, Glynneath, Neath and Rhigos years – let alone friends and family. I am not a public speaker, but I immensely enjoy private company, and the chat. Especially with the Rhigos crowd.

Yet, there was one public experience I really did enjoy. It was taking part in a dramatised film about a match between Wales and New Zealand.

It was a bit far-fetched since it was based on the idea of a touch judge admitting on his deathbed that he had cheated for Wales in the 1966 game between the two countries. So, according to the film's plot, the respective unions decided that twenty-five years after the incident, the game should be replayed, with the same players, at the Arms Park. I told you it was bit far-fetched, probably the result of a good afternoon session in an Auckland bar.

I know we seem to play the All Blacks every other month these days, but not too long ago they were infrequent events and hugely anticipated. People still refer to the controversial Wales vs All Blacks game in 1905, 107 years ago, which just goes to show the passion we have for the game and its controversies. I've no doubt that this film was inspired by the row that followed the 1905 game.

Personally, if a rugby drama or film had been made on a real incident, I would have relished the prospect of seeing the plot behind Andy Haden taking a dive from a line-out again as he did in 1978 when New Zealand were awarded a match winning penalty. No matter what was said after the game, and there was no lack of debate in the press, the general opinion is that Andy Haden, no stranger to controversy, deliberately fooled the referee Roger Quittenton, as he awarded that penalty when he and Frank Oliver 'fell' out of the line-out, and attracted the referee's attention. The resultant penalty by Fergie McCormick cost Wales the match, losing 13–12.

There was merry hell after the incident too. That same night, the Miss World competition was on the TV. The fantastic cartoonist, Gren of the *South Wales Echo*, captured the mood of Wales as he showed Miss New Zealand prostrate on the stage floor, claiming she had been 'pushed'.

That 'Haden fall' was a real incident, our drama was fictional. The film was also a comedy – couldn't have been anything else when you consider the cast included Windsor Davies. There were other sub-plots as well. An ageing New Zealand player had become a Salvation Army officer, and a love triangle had developed between some of the Welsh players and a woman. Another ex-All Black had become a corrupt politician. I was oblivious to the plots and drama, thank God, because I would never have understood them, but it was a great experience. Our only requirement was to play the game, under the coaching of All Black Steve McDowell.

The film was called *Old Scores* and it had some notable actors in it such as Robert Pugh, Dafydd Hywel, Dafydd Emyr, Glyn Houston and John Bach. But the rugby sequences of the 1966 game, filmed in 1991, involved genuine Wales and New Zealand players from the 1970s. I bet some of those ageing All Blacks went on diets and training before coming over and I bet our boys didn't. Thank goodness that most of us had non-speaking parts. Some of us by then had enough difficulty in learning line-out calls, let alone dramatic lines. The All Blacks team featured Ian Kirkpatrick, Waka Nathan, Alex Wyllie and Graham Thorne. All of us were dressed up in the kit of 1966, with Wales fielding Gerald Davies, Mervyn Davies, Gareth Edwards, Phil Bennett, the Pontypool front row, Dennis Hughes, Allan Martin, Mike Roberts, J.J. Williams – and me as a budding thespian. What company. Miner, me? No, thespian!

What was fantastic about the shoot was being able to sit down with the New Zealand boys and getting to know them. They were human. Ian Kirkpatrick, especially, was a great guy, and I think, no, I know, we went over the budget at the bar. We couldn't be paid for our theatrical effort because we were still governed by the old amateur regulations, but even Bobby Windsor was impressed by the expenses.

Some of us in the Welsh side were a little heavier and portly compared to our real international days, but not me. I was still packing down at 13 st. for Rhigos in 1991.

That same year, 1991, was my fiftieth birthday, and I celebrated it in Bermuda. I was part of the Welsh team taking part in the now well-established annual 'Classics' tournament.

Ironically, we had to play New Zealand, not the easiest of opponents, because though this was a friendly tournament, those boys still took it seriously – Andy Haden amongst them. There we were in a tropical paradise, and the All Blacks were still doing the haka as if their lives depended on it. They also had training sessions – serious ones too. We were in the bar.

I wonder if they ever relaxed.

There was a bit of bragging rights pride between England, Ireland and ourselves, but the All Blacks old boys had physios, game plans and frowns. We had Allan 'Panther' Martin as manager, who has by now probably qualified as a Bermudan citizen for all the tours he's taken there.

In the match against the All Blacks, I cracked a rib in one of the first tackles in the game. It was my fiftieth birthday present. It was also probably one of the last Bermuda classics to be enjoyed by international veterans. Very soon, players who had only been out of the limelight for a couple of months turned up, and it became a little serious. I think that is a pity, and though the social aspect is still good and the scenery fantastic, it has become too competitive.

We were veterans, and you could hardly say the same of some of the current teams travelling to Bermuda. Some of the players retire from international rugby and jump on the plane for the classics, though they are still involved in first-class rugby back home. Still, despite the cracked rib, I enjoyed my classics experiences.

Though the media gave me a wide berth during my career, and I gave them a wider one, I was still featured in one of the nationals. Through John Taylor I was approached by Pat Collins of the *Mail on Sunday*. He wanted to come to Rhigos, and only now do I know that it was all set up by J.T.

He was obviously an experienced interviewer because he got me to talk – not about my rugby career, but about Rhigos and the surrounding countryside, working in the mines and being a horse lover. When I get onto subjects like that, I don't stop. He published an article, which I thought was fair and to the point. But when the boys at Tower Colliery read it, I did take some leg-pulling. Yes, they deliver the *Mail on Sunday* even to Rhigos, as well as *The Morning Star*. When I read it, I couldn't believe I had told him so much.

8

Rhigos Rugby

I HAD ENJOYED my rugby, but I knew that my knee would never stand up to the challenges of top-class competition. Had my knee not taken so much of a wrenching, perhaps I could have added a few more caps to my total of thirty-four. Perhaps I should also have gone to the hospital for a check-up, but hospitals and I have never got on. They frighten me!

As far as I was concerned, Tommy David's tackle was hard but not dirty. I was just caught in an awkward position. If you play the game and are found in an exposed position, as I was, you pay the price. It was painful, and I knew it was serious.

After a summer of convalescence from rugby, though still working at Tower, I decided to give it one more go for Neath in a season opener against Penarth. It was no good, and I had to admit that the leg would not allow me the mobility I had once enjoyed. I left the field, confused, mixed up and pretty low.

The realisation that I could not play at the higher level was a huge disappointment. I had never sought the limelight, but I loved playing for Neath and Wales, and the company of the players and supporters. It was a massive part of my life. I didn't want to surrender, but probably because of my stubbornness and stupidity, by not seeking medical advice, I gave it all up. My stubbornness has been well documented by my family.

So I returned to Rhigos, working shifts at Tower Colliery, looking after Marlene, Greg and Helen, and the adopted animals.

Once the knee showed signs of recovery I played a few games as a guest for all the clubs around – Resolven, Cwmgwrach, Glynneath, Hirwaun – just to say thank you for all their support. But I had been talking to my mates in the village about starting up a Rhigos team for some time and we thought we might have the making of a village team. Most of my friends were playing for various clubs in the area. The pub chats at the Plough in Rhigos were enthusiastic, fuelled and loud, and some of those involved in the discussions are still officers of the club. God bless them – these are the true servants of Welsh rugby!

Graham Lewis began as secretary, and still holds that position, some forty years on. Clive Harris is still there, and Tom Tai Cwpla is still telling the same stories he was telling in the 1970s – though the stories have got better, larger and almost believable.

We talked about how we could do it. We didn't have anything but we had already secured some spare steel posts from Tower Colliery, and I'd hidden them in a local garage. It was a statement of ambition at least. Mind you, I insisted on doing a Saturday morning shift at Tower as payment for the posts. The only problem was that I was playing for Wales against England in Cardiff that afternoon, and the over-man at the colliery, Windsor Lewis, told me in no uncertain terms to get down to bloody Cardiff. At least I had the posts, and was down in Cardiff in plenty of time for a three o'clock kick-off.

Now we needed a field. We started playing our matches at Glynneath Welfare – a few miles down the road. We used a local restaurant, the Salad Bowl, as a clubhouse and we had the pithead baths at the neighbouring collieries as changing rooms. We stayed at Glynneath for a couple of seasons, always hoping that we might, one day, have a field in Rhigos.

We played our first game against Hirwaun 2nds. Ten tries scored but no conversions. Everybody seemed to have a go, so we knew we had to find an unemployed kicker somewhere. There had been a rugby side in Rhigos before, way back in the 1930s. It was originally a cricket team, and the members wanted to do something during the winter months. Some wanted to play football, others argued for rugby. The casting vote was sorted out by the local bobby – 'Evans the Police', and so Rhigos RFC was born, with a playing field behind the Plough Inn, a considerable uphill walk – and the opposition teams would complain that they were knackered before kick-off!

But that early rugby club was full of exemplary pioneers. They had a player's insurance scheme where they paid a £15 annual contribution into the Glynneath miners' welfare fund. Incredible, and so visionary! Unfortunately, the old club only lasted until the Second World War and folded.

So, here I am, a crocked international with great friends all around, but my village did not have a clubhouse, nor did we have a home pitch. We had a team and, eventually, we returned to the village and played on the school field. The Plough pub, for the time being, was our clubhouse, and to be in the Plough on match day was quite an event. Changing facilities were unique because we were given the use of the bath facilities at Tower and Aberpergwm collieries and Shands, the coal contractors. Twickenham and Murrayfield were already becoming distant memories.

We needed funds as well, and some of our money-raising ventures were a bit crude. I can recall a packed bingo session with numbers written on table tennis balls, and our tombola was a plastic shopping bag. All hell broke out when I shook the bag, and picked a number out and shouted "Six". "Fix!

Fix!" they shouted. How was I to know that it was a nine upside down and that six had already been called! There was pandemonium.

Later we had a '200' club, which quickly became the '500' club, and very soon there was something rather special happening and developing at Rhigos.

We had a nucleus of players who were all Rhigos boys, returning after playing for the neighbouring villages of Cwmgwrach, Resolven, Tonna, Hirwaun and Glynneath. Some were coming to the end of their careers, some in mid-career and we had a lot of young lads in the village who were keen to give it a go. Rhigos also had one crocked ex-international.

I am no organiser – Marlene and my closest friends would vouch for that – but there were great friends and enthusiasts around. Without Tom Tai Cwpla, Ken Grindle, Geraint and Eifion Jenkins, Graham and Clive and a whole host of others, we would not have made it. We had a committee of fifteen, and twenty-nine vice-presidents. Typical Welsh democracy!

Forget the Five Nations memories – this was the happiest period ever. My debt to Rhigos!

I have never enjoyed myself better than being part of that reborn Rhigos Rugby Club. I am still there on Saturdays watching Rhigos in division 5, south central, and on Sundays watching the grandchildren beginning their careers. Anything to get them away from screens and thumb games.

Brian Thomas, Glyn Shaw, Clive Rowlands and the Neath boys were fantastic in their support for the new venture, but I valued the effort of the local boys and men even more. We were entertainers, especially after a game. We had some immense talent in that direction. Trevor 'the Plough' didn't charge us for our meetings, but he was onto a good thing behind the bar.

I was humbled by the united effort, and honoured to be

a part of it. Those who have been in similar circumstances would appreciate, whether in Wales, Scotland, Fiji, Bermuda – or bloody anywhere – you are as good as your support and Rhigos, the village, was superb – even though we had started playing in Glynneath.

I have spoken to countless English people who have never understood how villages in Wales within a five-mile circumference can sprout and support three rugby teams. When you think of the Gwendraeth, Lliw, Tawe, Neath, Cynon and the great Rhondda valleys – what a great rugby factory line they have been. And today, from north Wales, how blessed have we been with George North? My friend, the late Dewi Bebb. would have been proud of him.

For Rhigos, Brian Thomas, by now a very impressive weight, came up to play for a few missionary and invitational games, so did Glyn Shaw and a few of the Neath lads. Their support for this forgotten but now revived rugby village in the Cynon Valley was fantastic.

Clive Rowlands was another major supporter, bringing international XVs to Rhigos. We couldn't have done without them. International stars in Rhigos! They came and magically found Rhigos before anyone had thought of satnavs.

So why did they come? Ah, well! That is the comradeship you had with fellow players. Nearly all had come through the system – school, local club and then senior rugby. They would appreciate what a challenge we had in trying to establish a rugby club, and I might have mentioned Rhigos to a few of them on the way. We desperately wanted a rugby club, and we were determined to have one. Support from my fellow Welsh and Neath players was great, but how on earth were we going to do it?

We certainly didn't have any millionaire backers. The mines, apart from Tower had gone, the factories had come and gone, so what else was in store for the Rhigos area?

People were moving away to find work. Somehow, we would have to go it alone. It has always been the story of Rhigos. I do wonder sometimes if the running water around Rhigos produces a defiant streak in all of us. It does seem that the area constantly battles against the odds.

Rhigos was a coal-rich area, and had been ripe for opencast mining. Yet, the drift and deep mines by now, it was claimed, were deemed to be unproductive, and despite the valiant efforts of Arthur Scargill against the media machinery of Thatcher's number 10, the battle was lost to keep the mines open – apart from a colliery a few hundred yards from my home, Tower Colliery. Tower was our defiant symbol – and those who still worked there when closure threatened bought it with their own redundancy money.

It was a massive challenge, and after the deluge of news coverage of protests, picket lines, scabs, soup kitchens and support the miners campaigns, there was a positive story to report that the boys of Tower, Rhigos, Hirwaun, Aberdare, Cwmgwrach and all around were standing defiant – with their own money – and producing coal.

During the miners' strike, I still worked as a safety man, but gave a healthy weekly contribution to the miners' strike fund. Keeping the colliery safe was necessary, since we all eventually wanted to get back to work. Later, under the inspirational leader Tyrone O'Sullivan, the men made Tower work and for a good time it worked well. It kept them employed, whereas in other areas of Wales, mining, miners and mines were delivered to the history pages. It was also comforting to know that the man at the NCB who had secured my pay during rugby tours for Wales, Mr Phillips Weekes, was also the adviser to the Keep Tower Colliery Open project.

But a few years on came the realisation that the coal seams at Tower and those of neighbouring closed collieries were exhausted, and despite valiant attempts the inevitable decision was made to close. I left Tower in 1986. That was a major blow to the area, because even with a smaller workforce, Tower was still, when it closed, the main employer in the area.

That really was a sad day. I had some redundancy money and bought a field and some sheep. Don't ask why. It was impulsive. I also found a job at a local office equipment factory as a welder.

But the country still needed coal – and that meant an increase in opencast mining.

I have to confess that one of the main people behind opencast mining in south Wales is my old school friend and current employer, Dai Walters of Rhigos. He has had a major influence on my life and my infatuation with horses. He is also the owner and creator of Ffos Las Racecourse.

But, at that time, there were other helping hands for our rugby club project, and it was one of the opencast companies – Shands – who supported us in trying to build a clubhouse and a pitch. It also helped that the agents for Shands were Barry James and Colin Morris – my brother. Nothing like having close connections, is there?

Tom Tai Cwpla's father owned a farm and some buildings very near the village. Sadly, his parents died very young, and Tom sold a large chunk of the land to the British Coal Corporation or the NCB for opencast mining. A number of other farms had also been bought. But once the fields had been dug up for coal, they were then left as wasteland. We negotiated with the Coal Board, and Tai Cwpla's old field and two small flat-roofed houses were sold to us for £1.

Shands (with Colin on board) were then persuaded to put something back into the community as compensation for all the opencast disruption. They levelled the pitch, placed drainage underneath – and we still had those posts in the garage from Tower Colliery. The two cottages were reshaped into a single-storey clubhouse. To us this was Twickenham – HQ.

It was a start, but it would take time, so for the first season we stayed at the Plough. Meantime, Shands did up the cottages, and we supplied the fixtures, fittings and labour. It was a dream come true. The club was eventually opened in 1978 by Clive Rowlands with an international XV. What a night and morning that was!

From then on, the rugby club became the focus of the community, especially with the village pensiners who were made honorary members.

There was also another major breakthrough. We had entered the East Glamorgan and Rhondda district union as a junior side. Glynneath gave us a full 1st XV fixture in our first season, followed by Aberaman and Cwmgwrach, but largely we played 2nd XV rugby against local sides.

It didn't matter. We were on our way.

There were no leagues in those days, so it was a matter of phoning around for a game. We would play thirty-five games per season. The furthest we travelled was to Carmarthen Athletic, but our area was full of clubs, all of them with 2nd XVs. So off we went to Treherbert, Aberaman, Pontrhydyfen, Hirwaun, Mountain Ash, Cefn Coed, Merthyr – and at home games, some of the old boys from the Rhigos side of 1939 would turn up. That was great to see.

Eventually, we bought a second-hand bus in a Merthyr auction, and I nominated myself as the driver, which did not go down well with everyone because I had a reputation for being heavy on the throttle. "You're driving this thing as if it's a car," Tai Cwpla would say. "Slow down, mun."

But what we had you cannot buy. We had natural comics, songsters and a cabaret act! Win or lose – we would entertain. There were some riotous evenings and the less said about kung fu fights in G-strings featuring Glyn Shaw, Glyn Thomas, Micky Harris and Gareth Powell, the better. If the press had got to know who the participants were, Wales might have been short of a few internationals, and Rhigos might have been reported for ungentlemanly conduct. Clive Rowlands saw one of these impromptu 'shows' and left ashen-faced!

I would also take my own international/invitational XV to clubs in the area. Well, there were a few internationals, like Brian Thomas, Glyn Shaw and David Weaver, but the rest were Rhigos boys. I also wanted to say thank you to all the clubs who had supported us in our campaign to be recognised. We played at Ferndale, Cwmgwrach, Tonna, Resolven and a few others.

I took over the coaching and selection. We played in the original colours of the old club – black and amber. A local man, a Mr Howells, designed our badge, two bronze axes crossing, the local lake and a phoenix. The prehistoric axes, we had been told in school, had been unearthed and found in the locality; the lake was a local beauty spot, and our club was the phoenix rising from the ashes. As they say in Rhigos, "Impressive, innit?"

I think our finest moment was reaching the quarter-final of the Welsh Brewers Cup. Our opponents were Butetown in Cardiff, a team we had already beaten that season.

We lost, and to this day, Clive Harris, our captain, blames me. I had the line in my sight for a winning try in extra time, but decided to pass the ball to our wing Jeff Roberts.

Out of nowhere came a try-saving tackle from Danny Wilson, an extremely talented ex-Cardiff player and father of Ryan Giggs. Clive insists that Rhigos lost that game because I wasn't selfish enough. But our appearance and success in that competition meant that we could mingle with the best of the second-class clubs.

I knew my playing time was coming to an end, but there was one ambition left.

Greg was developing into a very good player at youth level. He was already taller and heavier than me as well! He had already been invited to a Welsh youth trial, and he had also attracted the attention of the French club Brive, and went out there. Unfortunately, the promises made were not kept, and he returned home. So I just wanted to play a few games with him for Rhigos in the back row. We achieved that a few times, and he was on the field with me at Cwrt Herbert in Neath when I cracked my ribs and finished my Rhigos career.

Well, not quite finished! Allan Martin was in charge of the Welsh golden oldies team in the Bermuda classics, and I played in two tournaments out there, damaging my ribs again.

Some of the Rhigos boys, a little younger than me, had also started to play veterans rugby. There weren't many fixtures, and they were not particularly hard games, but the temptation proved too much. There were games against Bromsgrove, Bromyard and Wednesbury, and there were a few local teams such as Ferndale Vets.

The boots were always to be found, now hidden in the shower room, and I would turn up to see if the veterans were short. I would also volunteer if Rhigos were short as well, because I didn't like to see Rhigos take to the field with fourteen men.

The final act of my rugby career was a major disappointment. I had put together a XV from the local clubs, including Rhigos, to play against a Welsh Charitables XV, a body that raises much needed money for various charities in Wales under the guidance of the hard-working David Power.

It was a great occasion for me, being able to contribute and do something. I agreed to run the line, if I was allowed to come on in the second half for a cameo appearance. It was the last time I wore the Rhigos colours and a pair of boots. I pulled a bloody hamstring running the line, and couldn't play. I couldn't believe it! It was September 1998 – I was fifty-seven years old.

9

Racing

Introduction by Richard Evans

THERE WAS A knock on the door at our home in Stratford. If memory serves me correctly, it was a Sunday afternoon. I opened the door and immediately recognised him.

Dai Morris, a legend in my books, was standing there with Marlene, his wife. This was bizarre. They had seen our sign outside the farm stating that we were horse breeders. They were, of course, invited in and, frustratingly, all I wanted to do was talk about Welsh rugby, and all he wanted to do was talk about horses.

My background, which he didn't know at that time, was west Wales – Bancyfelin, birthplace of Delme Thomas and the current Wales scrum half, Mike Phillips.

So here I am, in my front room, with a man I had huge respect for, but he just wanted to know whether he could bring his mare, Princess Glory who'd had no success on the tracks, to breed with one of my stallions. I couldn't say no. Normally, I might have. But this was Dai Morris.

It was the start of a great friendship, not particularly beneficial in financial terms for Dai, since those foals came to nothing for racing. But a stallion I sold to the wonderful

Rhigos village syndicate made some amends. Not much, but they did allow me into Rhigos.

What a genuine, unassuming man, who would listen to anything about the horse world. We became great friends, and I always seek his company at the Ffos Las Racecourse. If there was a reward for passion, he would have been a top breeder. As a man I have met few better.

There was one occasion when I was down in Cardiff with two mates for an international. I asked Dai, now long retired from rugby, if he could help us find tickets. Before the match he gave us three tickets. To this day, I think they were his personal ones, and he probably stayed in the Angel Hotel to watch the match on television.

What a man! I have the utmost regard for him. I just wish he'd had more success with the horses. He did with Helen's Vision, but his dedication deserved more.

Richard Evans
Former jockey and top horse breeder

*   *   *

There were always horses roaming around Rhigos. Our neighbours and closest friends Mr and Mrs Gregory had Welsh cobs next door, as well as Crufts-standard Welsh terriers. My father and Uncle Jack had ponies. Nearly all the farmers and smallholders had horses, and there were wild ones on the Beacons as well.

So it was only natural that I had an affinity with horses from the very beginning, being able to proudly drive Mr Gregory's pony and cart around the village, to the halcyon days of being in the owners' enclosure at Newbury and Aintree. Worth more than a Welsh cap that. Well, almost.

I also enjoyed betting, not large sums of money, but I would follow form, trainers, jockeys and yards. It was a fascination from very early on. My father loved pigeon and greyhound racing. But I took to horses. I followed the results with the same fanaticism as some follow their football and rugby teams. Some might have thought that I was a compulsive gambler, since I frequently disappeared to the bookies wherever I was. But I wasn't. It was a hobby, and I longed for the day when I could own a racehorse and be a part of that scene. Not the fancy dress and *crachach* stuff, but the thrill of being a horse owner. At the time, it was crystal-ball gazing. How does a pitman become a racehorse owner?

My best ever betting return was a £1 each way bet on Mon Mome in the 2009 Grand National. It came in at 100–1 and the only reason I backed it was because Liam Treadwell was the jockey, and he had ridden for me. Yes, me! David Morris, owner, Rhigos, Mid Glamorgan. It is in the books.

Yes, ownership or being involved in horse racing was always my dream. It was a very ambitious dream on colliery wages, as I found out.

I confess that if Neath had an away game at London Welsh, Bath or Gloucester, I would naturally study form at Bath, Newbury, Chepstow or the Cheltenham racecourses. Don't ask me why – probably just because I was in the vicinity. Daft, plain daft!

Luck plays a major part in horse racing. But it was my good fortune that Brian Thomas, my fellow Neath player and skipper, had been to Cambridge University, and one of his contemporaries was Ian Balding. Brian was always well connected, and he was Ian's 'best man'. Ian Balding, like Brian, was also a Cambridge Blue, so he must have been a fairly good player. His daughter, Clare, knows her stuff too! There was some advice on tap.

I then met Richard Evans, a professional jockey turned horse breeder, at Stratford, and that was the beginning of an enduring friendship. It was Richard who really sent me on my horse racing pathway. It was quite a journey, and though there were a number of moments of despair and disappointment, there was also great joy and excitement.

Yet the biggest influence on my equestrian journey has to be Dai Walters – or Gweirydd as he was known as a boy in Rhigos. I am totally indebted to him, and am still involved in looking after his horses in Lisvane, Cardiff. Apart from owning horses, Dai also owns Ffos Las Racecourse in west Wales which he built on an old opencast coal site, after amassing a huge fortune through his civil engineering and mining companies. He even built gallops into the side of Caerphilly Mountain near his house in Cardiff.

His story should be told sometime too, because he started out working with one bulldozer and a mate on small local contracts and, over the years, his plant hire, civil engineering and opencast activities have become one of the most impressive industrial success stories of Wales. Dai is now one of the wealthiest people in the country. He identifies land for potential development, so I'm told, when flying around in his helicopter. Yet his devotion to horses and racing is also legendary and crucial to the Welsh horse racing industry. Anyone will tell you that owning racehorses is a financial drain, especially when only 10 per cent of the owners win. You then have to deduce that the 90 per cent of us lesser people do it for pleasure. That's me!

Dai and I were at school together in Rhigos primary, and neither of us could be classed as academic. Ken Grindle reckons that we were the foundations of the school, since everybody else was above us. Dai invited me to go and work for him at his stables. For that, I will be eternally grateful. You have no idea what that meant to me. An unemployed collier and welder being invited into an arena where my obsession could be fulfilled.

Between the Rhigos show being held outside my home, the point-to-point races, Mr Gregory's cobs and just about every farmer owning a few ponies, it was inevitable that I should end up on a stable yard somewhere. But Dai's invitation meant that I could do what I had always wanted to do, for the rest of my life. And to work for a Rhigos man as well.

I am not sure what really sparked off my interest in the 'turf' or racing. Yet it does seem that I have spent more than a lifetime reading and listening to anything involved with racing, especially hurdling and jumps. I'd hang around for hours outside the Rhigos bookie, with my young daughter Helen patiently – or sometimes not – waiting outside.

My father was obsessive as well – but he chose pigeons – and stood still outside, waiting hours for them to return. I couldn't do that.

Racing got a hold on me, there's no doubt about that, and the racing pages of any newspaper were well thumbed on a daily basis.

I am sure that some of the Neath and Welsh boys thought I was a compulsive gambler – far from it. They didn't complain or pass comment when I helped them out. Who was it that they turned to when we went horse racing in Dunedin, New Zealand or here in the UK – and ask for tips? Me! I went round the Dunedin parade ring during the 1969 Welsh tour and chose a few horses which I thought were well prepared. The race card also helped which they, as the prime of Welsh rugby playing and intellectual talent, didn't understand at all, and I picked out a few likely contenders.

By the end of the afternoon the entire squad were my closest friends. With a bit of luck and a bit of knowledge, there were suddenly Welsh players with wads of cash in their hands. I don't think I had a punt myself. In all honesty, if I was that good a tipster I would be as rich as my mate Dai Walters, but I am not.

I am not a financial genius either. If I had known how much money this horse ownership business would entail, and the twists and emotional turns it would bring, I might have been dissuaded. Marlene kept the books, and kept telling me how expensive everything was – 'a bloody fortune' – but I was stubbornly deaf. It was an ambition I had harboured. It is difficult to explain, but in a country full of train spotters, stamp collectors and football fanatics this, too, was a compulsive, innocent obsession. There were no trains to spot in Rhigos anyway.

Eventually Marlene gave in. I'd been talking about it for years. A decision was made. The whole family went to the Ascot sales, kids and all, to see what was available, affordable and acceptable. Helen loved every animal, and we could have bought the lot if she had her way! Eventually we bought Princess Glory, a two-year-old mare, the darling of the family, and we took her to a local trainer Derrick Haydn Jones at Efail Isaf, just outside Cardiff.

Naturally, there was huge anticipation as we took her flat racing at Windsor, Bath and Chepstow. Alas, our anticipation was matched by our disappointment, because she didn't feature at all, and we knew that the only hope for her was to breed.

That is when I met Richard Evans. Again there was disappointment as nothing came of her foals either. She was brought home to Rhigos, and Helen adored her. She stayed with us on the field outside and eventually died at the age of twenty-three. She is buried in the field, not too far from where we also buried Helen's 30-year-old pony, and the rest of our pets who have died, buried around the back. That particular day was very sad.

It didn't diminish my enthusiasm though; I was now

really attracted to this horse-owning business. It had severely dented my limited finances, and I realised that if I had a future in horse-racing ownership, I would need help. It was on the doorstep.

It must have shaken the British horse racing world to hear of the newly-formed Rhigos syndicate! It was created when we were in the process of building the Rhigos clubhouse. It was a social crew, to say the least – not one of these big syndicates that sprout from the City of London with well-to-do financiers. Our commitment to, and enthusiasm for the horse-racing business increased in the late hours of socialising at the Rhigos clubhouse! We were going to take Aintree, Cheltenham and Ascot by storm! Can you imagine the chat?

This, for us, was the big time and depending on the hour of day, we had big ambitions. There were ten of us. Some were local, some had family in Rhigos and some had extremely tenuous connections with the area. The syndicate team included Aubrey Butt, Dave Power, a colliery mate, known to all as 'Taxi' Penwaun, Jimmy Lewis, John Probert from Hirwaun, my brother-in-law John Davies, Colin, my brother, Tom Tai Cwpla, Brendan Hogan and my new horse-breeder friend and ex-jockey from Stratford, Richard Evans.

The syndicate-owned horse was called St Dubasoff, a two-year-old stallion bought from Richard Evans, and if enthusiasm counted for anything, it would have won the Cheltenham Gold Cup. Well, it didn't win that trophy, but we did taste some success.

Although we paid a fortune on a monthly basis for three years in trainer's fees, feed, transport and everything else, our return didn't match the costs. I still have the records of the training feeds, £590, £390, £487, £567 – and the vet, blacksmith, jockey and entry fees. Well, they were something else as well.

It did not start very well at all, but after being 'cut', there was a vast improvement. It won two-mile hurdle races at Worcester and Exeter, but apart from a third and fifth place, that was it. The winnings were shared out, leaving all of us well out of pocket. Matters got worse: St Dubasoff, with a broken tendon, had to be put down on the way home from a race meeting.

I still hear, to this day, mutterings about that 'investment'. "Should have popped him over Rhigos Mountain" or "bound for dog food tins, that one" – I heard them all. After that experience I don't think I could get another Rhigos-based syndicate going.

But if you believe, then sometimes, things happen.

Dai Walters had bought Celtic Major, a super horse, and it was being trained by Jonjo O'Neill. Unfortunately it had a hairline fracture, and needed box rest for six months at the Hollies, in Lisvane, Cardiff, where Dai lived and had his stables – and where I was now working.

It needed company and Dai had a look around for a horse to share the box. By chance after a chat at a local pub, the Maenllwyd near Lisvane, he met Tim Jones, who had a bay yearling that he had bought for 600 guineas which would do the job.

We went to have a look at the horse. Like all yearlings it didn't look like much, but fine for the task in hand. I have to admit that I really took to this horse from day one, and looked after it as if she was my own. There was something about her. For some six months I was there every day, as well as attending to Celtic Major. I did wonder if Mr Jones would sell it to me, so I asked Dai for some advice. "Go and tap him up," he told me. I am not very good at that type of thing. Mr Jones wanted £1,500 for the horse. That to me was real money. There was one other factor to consider. How would Marlene react? We'd had a few robust discussions after the

Princess Glory episode. But I must have caught her at a weak moment because, incredibly, she said yes – and the deal was done.

Gradually the horse got stronger and I have to confess that I was now totally devoted to it. Dai Walters has always said that I am far too soft, and he reckons I would be a bad trainer, prone to overfeeding the horses.

When Celtic Major was pronounced fit, they were both turned out. My horse had already put on weight and was beginning to look the part. She was small, just a little bigger than a pony really, but her coat was superb.

It was Helen, my daughter, who had a look at my 'pet' and said "I think you have a winner there, Dad!" From there on, the horse was christened Helen's Vision. The irony, in all of this, was the discovery that our Helen, who was devoted to horses from a very young age, even riding Brian Thomas's horses, was allergic to them. Her allergy got worse as she got older with severe asthmatic bouts. It was so frustrating for her, since she desperately wanted to be with us, the family, as we headed up and down the country with Helen's Vision in tow in a horsebox and me driving.

Another Helen, Helen Lewis, a former point-to-point champion, was a trainer on Dai's yard as Helen's Vision took to the gallops. She was a small horse, but I also knew that she was made of sturdy stuff, and certainly had character. She always wanted to lead. Add to that, with the generosity of Dai Walters, she had one of the finest equipped stables and yards in the country to encourage her training and recovery. When ready, she would run in the Walters colours, because I didn't have a licence.

On her national hunt flat debut, we were all there at Huntingdon. There was huge excitement and nervous anticipation. Was she good enough or, as Marlene would say, "What a waste of money"? She was beaten by a short head, coming second, and third, notably, was Dai's horse Tonto. Good bragging rights on the yard for Monday morning! This was unbelievable from a horse that a few months earlier was not even strong enough to be a pet pony. But I knew that she had spirit – loads of it. Then we went to Warwick, where she was beaten by a horse that had cost thousands of pounds.

The family were now really engaged, and a lifelong ambition of owning a real winner was not so far-fetched.

It happened at Stratford in a two-mile national hunt flat race with Liam Treadwell on board. I stood and stared – that was all I could do. You can't imagine the pride. Those jibes from the village boys about St Dubasoff being fit for dog food were long forgotten. I think I grew a few inches above my playing height as well when walking around Rhigos. Helen's Vision had already paid back my investment.

It happened again and she won at Newbury over two miles. Helen Lewis, the trainer at Dai's yard, was having great success. I was beginning to enjoy the taste of success as well – Helen's Vision was the talk of Rhigos.

There was one race left on our schedule, at Aintree of all places, a two-mile listed national hunt flat race. No joy there as she came fourth. But we were very pleased after that first season. I also had to pinch myself. I had been in the Aintree owners' enclosure.

We then started preparing her for the next national hunt season under the careful eye of Helen. Dai Walters thought she might do better over hurdles. I expressed my doubts because I didn't want her hurt. But it wasn't about me.

It was the logical progression. She would now also run in my own colours. Owner: W.D. Morris! It would not surprise you to know that my colours were red for Wales and black for Neath.

My name had been in rugby programmes before, but I was

now in the racing world books and form guides alongside some legendary names in the racing world. I just couldn't believe it. My name would now be heard over the tannoy at the Rhigos bookie!

We took her to Newbury for her first novice hurdle race, full of nervousness and excitement. We could hardly have expected such a result. She won, beating fifteen other horses by twenty-seven lengths, at a price of 9–2 as third favourite. This, from the scrawny animal I had almost hand fed back to health. I cried. I don't think I was alone.

I think it was here that an Irish horse breeder approached Dai Walters about Helen's Vision. I'm told he offered £150,000 for her, there and then. Canny, the Irish, they know their horses, and a bit about rugby too. Dai told him that I was the owner of the horse, and he should take his offer to me.

Helen Lewis, also took a call from Ireland. It was another offer.

That kind of money would have solved a fair number of problems around Rhigos, but there was no way we were going to part company. I didn't even consider it, or discuss it, even when Dai offered £50K for part ownership. Why, did I need the money anyway?

"Take the money for the mare," said Dai "you've had a good run with her, and she'll breed well."

I wouldn't listen. Looking back, perhaps I should have. But we were so emotionally attached to her, and I don't think Helen Lewis would have approved either. Helen's Vision was a part of her as well as our family. We had invested too much time and care – let alone money.

We couldn't wait for the next season. Newbury was something of a favourite track for us. She won a two-mile novice hurdle, and followed that up with a third and a fourth on the Newbury course. She was also attracting a bit of attention in the racing press as well. That last race also signalled the end of the training partnership, since Helen Lewis left the Hollies yard. She had been remarkable.

Helen's Vision was taken to a new, up-and-coming Welsh trainer in Cowbridge. Tim Vaughan had been a successful show jumper and point-to-pointer, and had the enthusiasm to match his ambitions.

There were races around the country where she didn't feature. Cheltenham, Wincanton, Bangor, Ascot and Sandown, but Tim entered her for a listed handicap hurdle at Newbury. She won, giving Tim and me our first listed winner. Incredible!

Two third places followed at Doncaster, and her overall track record showed that in twenty-eight outings she had won four races, and in addition had been placed in seven others. My 'pet' had more than rewarded my initial care of her.

She was trained for her last few races by Andrew Boxall at the Walters yard. Nothing in this racing world is predictable, as I was about to find out. We made a decision. She was sent to the local Dunraven Stud for breeding, but alas, the vets discovered that she was short of ovaries, and wouldn't catch. So there would be no foals. This was a colossal disappointment as you can imagine for all of us. That would have sorted out the bank balance for years. There was little we could do but try her out on the tracks again. We sent her to James Evans at Worcester, the brother of Richard Evans. She ran three races for him, coming in fifth in one race, but making little impact beyond that.

It seemed to us that she performed promisingly well in the first or second outing with each new trainer, but sadly the form after that was disappointing as well as puzzling.

Something was amiss, so we sent her down for a couple of months to John Flint at Kenfig Hill to assess the problem. John was an experienced trainer, and it wasn't long before he responded – and it was not good news.

John discovered that every time she raced on the gallops, she was breaking blood vessels, and from there on the story of Helen's Vision took a downward turn. She couldn't race again.

She had been such an amazing, valiant character, and she had fulfilled my ambition. I had been to places and racecourses that I had heard of in the Rhigos bookie and read about in the *Racing Post*, and I had now lived the dream. Dai kindly allowed me to leave her to graze at the Hollies in Lisvane when she was brought home.

Would I do it again? I don't think so. The amount of money required is daunting, and I don't think I could cope with the disappointment and turmoil again. But you never know. I know it won't be up to me, but Mrs Marlene Morris. Helen's Vision was a one-off.

If that had been the end of my association with horses, it would have been very hard to take. Fortunately, at the Hollies there are horses coming and going all the time, trainers and jockeys to talk to. The horses Celtic Major and the Celtic string of horses, Snoopy Loopy, Grand Slam Hero, Oscar Whisky, and a host of others, have all been successful for Dai, success that he richly deserves.

But when Dai decided to start building his own racecourse at Ffos Las in Trimsaran, just outside Llanelli, that was a pretty sensational and challenging period. I am not sure how much support he received from the racing fraternity, since there were a number of doubters around, especially when another new racecourse development, Great Leigh's in Essex, ran into planning and financial trouble.

To turn a 600-acre opencast coal site into a premier-class racecourse was some challenge, but as the racecourse began to take shape, I would be asked to take down a horse or two for the press photo shoots.

Dai Walters from Rhigos is nothing if not resilient, and

perhaps I should have listened to him, and accepted the big money offers for Helen's Vision. If Dai Walters is resilient, this Dai is just plain stubborn. Ask the kids! But I am sure that Dai had a few doubtful moments during that development period. Some questioned the location, since it is not a densely populated area. It was also some way from the M4 and access was difficult, but I come back to that Rhigos defiance.

Whatever the difficulties, they were tackled. Ffos Las is a major asset to west Wales and Welsh racing.

I had my time; it was exhilarating, expensive and enjoyable. I am still, at the age of seventy, amongst horses, owners, jockeys and trainers. My short association with the top end of the industry was a fantastic journey, and I have met some great people. Helen's Vision had a great deal to do with that. She is now grazing on one of Dai's fields in Cowbridge, and I still see her every other day. She was something else.

10

Playing
with Gareth

AT THE RISK of offending all my ex-playing colleagues, especially those at Neath, I think it would be wrong of me not to single out Gareth Edwards for a special mention. Gareth was special to Wales and the British Lions, and a role model for any aspiring scrum half. He, quite simply, had it all.

I played with and against some extremely talented Welsh scrum halves: Martyn Davies, Dai Parker, Clive Shell, Chico Hopkins, Selwyn Williams and my Rhigos friend Clive Harris.

But Gareth was special. We won our first caps together, and though we hardly discussed tactics or game plans for any of my thirty-six caps, we knew each other inside out. It was my mission to track him wherever he went – though that sounds a bit too simple. Gareth could go into areas of play from his position that were unchartered.

Opponents got to know him, and they had a pretty good idea what he was going to do. And they still couldn't stop him. Even his first international try against France in 1969 featured pace, determination and power. He left some bruises on those Frenchmen to announce his scoring potential. Fifty-three consecutive caps in eleven years and twenty tries later – he was still bruising people with those fierce darts over the gain line.

I first saw him play as a schoolboy for Millfield School against Neath Grammar School. He looked something special that day as well, and I know he owes and acknowledges a huge debt of gratitude to his teacher Bill Samuel at Pontardawe Tech. Gareth had wanted to play centre, but Bill told him that he would never make the local under-15 team in that position. Bill told him to play scrum half because he could kick, run and pass.

At the beginning, when we first met each other, I didn't know really what to expect, since he, too, as a 19-year-old Cardiff Training College student was learning the ropes, and as a 5' 8", 11 st. 9 lb scrum half, he was more of an athlete than the all-rounder he was to become. As a schools champion hurdler and long jumper, he had perfected that explosive start, so I began to learn where and when he might launch and spring himself into a sprint from a standing start. If I was wrong, I'd be well behind.

It happened once, when he scored that incredible try in the mud against Scotland. I know he tells people in his dinner speeches that he was looking around for me and that I had abandoned him, but I was still engaged in having a 16 st. Scottish lock forward holding onto me. Not that he would have passed anyway!

His delivery at the beginning was accurate and short, often a dive pass, before he mastered his spin pass technique. I think that developed when he first saw what Sid Going could achieve. It placed Barry and Phil yards away from the opposing back rows, and the old laws didn't allow the midfield traffic jams of the modern game. It gave them, and the people outside, like John Dawes and Arthur Lewis, space to negotiate and exploit, and that was largely down to Gareth's technical mastery from the base.

He was made captain of Wales at the age of twenty, when there were some very seasoned players around him. His early captaincy didn't faze him personally at all, but I think it did affect his play. He took too much on, but gradually the maturity developed unbelievably. It took a couple of seasons for us to appreciate what a complete armoury of skills he possessed. His height didn't alter, but his power and weight did.

He ran low at pace, and eventually had the upper frame of a formidable loose forward with the speed of a wing. Against him, you had to stop him at base, because once into his stride he could pulverise any defence.

I well remember Brian Thomas in a Neath changing room telling us: "Stop Edwards and John and you stop Cardiff."

Gareth's kicking also became a formidable asset. He was a master of the ball, and it came as no surprise to learn that he had been offered a contract at Swansea Town as a youngster. Those long raking defensive kicks into enemy territory were soul destroying for the attacking sides, and pretty challenging to chase as well.

In defence he took some punishment, but had the build to withstand the pressure. I find it quite remarkable that he never suffered from any bone fractures, not even a cut during his entire career. Must have been well protected! A vote for the backroom boys there, I think!

We couldn't protect his hamstrings though. That was up to Gerry Lewis, the physio, and the two of them were hardly apart. An X-ray of Gareth's hamstrings should be shown at the National Museum of Wales – alongside Owain Glyndŵr's crest and armoury. They were that important to the nation. Just ask him, if you've got an hour or two to spare!

Protection – that was our role. He was indispensable to the Welsh cause. So, too, were Barry and Phil. But Gareth was the catalyst.

I always enjoyed the story of when a young Gareth played against Clive Rowlands at St Helens, with Gareth sniping around the scrum as a cheeky young scrum half, and diving between Clive's legs for a try. Clive was not the fastest scrum half on the planet. Gareth was. I could listen to that story all night, and just watch 'Top Cat's' face.

But Gareth had no side to him. By that I mean he was never a breath away from his Gwauncaegurwen roots and his father's mining background, although I know he went to Millfield, a top school. He, like Gerald, was only a generation away from the pits. He respected all of us who delivered on the field of play – the steelworker, teacher, electricity linesman – and whatever else those London Welsh boys did for a living!

Gareth and Barry communicated in Welsh on the field; thank goodness Mervyn and I had been brought up in a Welsh-speaking environment. We sort of knew what was being planned behind, but their ability to improvise and play off the cuff left many a plan on the drawing board. That was true of Gareth and Phil Bennett as well. If the opposition found it difficult to track Benny's sidestepping path, imagine what it was like to follow him.

I think, looking back, that Barry's sudden retirement from the game allowed Gareth to take more responsibility on the field. Barry always wanted the ball because he always claimed that he could see more of the game than Gareth.

Barry retired, and in stepped Phil Bennett – a different magician. Gareth took more of the tactical responsibilities from the base, and didn't exploit the talents we had behind until he was content that the battle up front was tilting our way. And what a competitive conductor he was. The very best player of all.

11

Dai Morris
XV vs World XV
An Indulgence

IT'S BEEN A privilege to be asked to play in some great invitational XVs. Although they are brought together for something special like a clubhouse opening, a charity or an anniversary, you can't let your guard down in these matches.

The ones I really enjoyed were the games I played in when I was well into my forties. The expectation was lower, not for me, but from the supporters. So I am going to indulge myself, and select two teams, a Welsh XV, containing players I have played with, and an international or world XV, of players I have opposed.

I will confess, and I am sure that the Rhigos committee would probably nod, that I am not very good at selection – but only because I don't really want to leave anyone out!

I can tell you that selecting these two teams has kept me awake for a few nights. I have stared at a blank piece of paper for weeks, because every nomination, especially in the international XV, would have at least half a dozen contenders. I can also think of a great team of Welsh players who were never capped. I look forward to the response from Rhigos Brains Trust. Knowing that lot they will probably disagree on every one. But it will be a good night of debate.

The Welsh team of the 1970s was successful, and there will be no major surprises in most of my selections because I have no desire at present to leave the country or be sent to Coventry. I also think we were denied seeing the best of some players when they went north. I'm thinking in particular of Maurice Richards, Keith Jarrett, Terry Price, Glyn Shaw and John Mantle. John Mantle's departure did leave the back row slots open to competition, allowing myself, Ron Jones, John Jeffrey, Bobby Wanbon, Mervyn, John Taylor and later Tommy David to stake our claims.

But, as I have mentioned before, that 1970s team was more like a club team. There may have been the odd dropout because of injury, but it was largely a settled side, and we got to know each other as we were developed by Clive Rowlands and skippered by John Dawes. It was also Clive's good fortune to have such a group of players, much the same as Warren Gatland has now. As a small nation these tides of talented players come so often, but not often enough for the faithful and fanatical supporters.

I have yet to understand how New Zealand, with the same population as Wales, can consistently provide exceptional teams. I have never seen a bad New Zealand side. They have been beaten, but by and large, rugby standards are set by them.

Clive provided Welsh pride and passion, but the real work was not done on Aberavon beach. It was done quietly and thoughtfully by a Newbridge man, an ex-UCW Aberystwyth student playing in Richmond, Surrey. The foundation of that 1970s team was undeniably London Welsh, and the influence of John Dawes was immense.

Just think of this list: John Dawes himself, Jim Shanklin, Gerald Davies, Mike Roberts, Geoff Evans, John Taylor,

Mervyn Davies, Tony Gray, and if I leave out J.P.R., I'll probably need a knee job – which, by the way, is long overdue.

When you played against these guys at the Gnoll or Old Deer Park, it was like meeting the Harlem Globetrotters with studs on. They ran everything.

My team is pretty much London Welsh-based, which will upset those boys at the Gnoll. The one man I feel for who should have been given the opportunity to express himself was Glen Ball of Neath. He should have moved to London Welsh! He was a complete footballer.

I've also left out the outstanding Brian Price. So that will be one Christmas card missing next year.

My full back in the Dai Morris XV is of course J.P.R. Williams. John was a stalwart in defence and always looking for the counterattacking opportunity. He might not have been the best kicker of the ball, in the mould of our Grahame Hodgson, but he was extremely competitive, which I liked. In fact, I think he was the most competitive of us all. And who will forget his drop goal for the Lions in 1971? No one in ear shot anyway.

My right wing has to be the son of a miner, with a very long name. No wonder Thomas Gerald Reames Davies was known as T.G.R. He was 'Ger' to us, 'Reames' to the London Welsh boys, and a great fellow traveller. Educated, mind you, Cambridge and all that, but never aloof. He was Llansaint through and through. What a finisher! He was an inspiration to all – just ask Shane Williams.

He is now on the International Rugby Board. He is also a WRU member. He is by no means what I have called a blazer in this book, but I suspect that he has his work cut out trying to sort out the other blazers.

I've pondered a lot about the other wing position. There was John Bevan, a massive presence with attitude. Few could wrestle with him, and he went north. J.J. Williams was an exceptionally fast sprinter, and he perfected the kick and chase scoring opportunity. But to me, Maurice Richards was outstanding.

He was a Lion in 1968. His movement with pace terrified you in opposition, but as a team-mate, he was exceptional. You didn't think he could do some of the things that he did. He'd skin an opponent in front of your eyes with shifts of deceptive speed, and had a zest for the try line.

The two centres are John Dawes and Arthur Lewis. I have yet to see two better passers of the ball, even in the modern game. I admire the thrust of Jamie Roberts and the fantastic physical drive of the Scarlet centres, Jonathan Davies and Scott Williams. I would have loved to play alongside them. They have that vision to 'pop' inside. I also admired the individual sidestepping brilliance of D.K. Jones, totally laid-back, before pulsating into action. Then along came Mark Ring and Bleddyn Bowen. I would have loved to have played with them all. Each one of them had the ability to do something exceptional.

In terms of my contemporary players, 'Sid' Dawes and Arthur were fantastic. They knew that in Gerald, Maurice, John Bevan and J.J. Williams they had finishers. Few passes were wasted, they also created space and Arthur, so often, did the damage with that initial thrust, as 'Sid' orchestrated behind. There was always space to be developed in our game from the set pieces, which unfortunately is not the case today. You now have to wait for phased possession and delivery.

So now the major dilemma! The gliding operator – or the jinking impresario: Barry John or Phil Bennett. It is a very tough call. Both were key players. I could opt out here from voting, because they were both so instrumental in guiding Wales to slams, crowns and championships.

From my position, as a so-called 'shadow', I loved to play

with Barry. He glided with two hands on the ball, something I would like to impose an all youngsters. He had such a feel for the game and, as a pretty good snooker player, he worked out the angles.

But Benny could sidestep around a sixpence, and he was at his best launching something out of nothing from defence, leaving opposition, and indeed sometimes his support, flat footed. He, too, was a man with snooker abilities. I wonder if that had something to do with it, and of course they both loved their football too.

They were Lions. Both were exceptional. In terms of being a support player, as I was, I have opted for Barry. That is another Christmas card gone. I hate this!

But I have no such hesitation in the front row. I have never met anyone as strong or as resilient as Glyn Shaw. I saw him at work, I saw him at Neath, and he was by some distance the strongest man I have never known on a rugby field. He too went north – and was much missed by Welsh rugby.

Nor have I met a man more resilient than John Lloyd. These guys were not the celebrated heroes. This was the machine room of the team.

Jeff Young would be my hooker. Many underestimated Jeff, but he was tough and mobile, and an excellent ball carrier with some pace. Bobby Windsor was a mighty no-nonsense presence as well, but I think it was only when he was later joined by Charlie Faulkner and Graham Price that we saw the best of Bobby. Norman Gale was around in my time too, and he'd never take a step back.

Delme, my friend from Llanelli, and my team captain at Neath, Brian Thomas, take the second row. The first, because I have not met a stronger front-of-the-line jumper, and he had immense strength in retaining the ball until it was time to release. That could also be said of Brian, one of the best maulers and disruptive players around. Few relished a confrontation with Twmws, and the fact that he was selected out of position in the front row against the All Blacks speaks volumes. There was, of course, the immense high aerial supremacy of Ben Price of Newport, but when the going got tough on the ground, that is where you would find Brian Thomas. He was an uncompromising character and now sadly missed.

My back row naturally features John Taylor and the late Mervyn Davies. Two of the finest players, with significant abilities, and very different from my own. The back of the line-out was, in that era, often busier than the second or front rows, because that is where we attacked and supported.

My own position goes to Tommy David. With ball in hand and a few years to get going, there were few who could top him. It is a selection that might anger a few Gnoll folk, because of the tackle which finished my first-class career, and in opposition with Llanelli, Tommy was a handful.

I have left out a number of good players – Denzil Williams, Barry Llewelyn, Terry Cobner, Derek Quinnell and a whole host of backs. Perhaps I should start again.

So this is my team:

15. J.P.R. Williams
14. T.G.R. Davies
13. John Dawes [c]
12. Arthur Lewis
11. Maurice Richards
10. Barry John
9. Gareth Edwards
1. Glyn Shaw
2. Jeff Young
3. John Lloyd
4. Delme Thomas
5. Brian Thomas

6. Tommy David
7. John Taylor
8. Mervyn Davies

In choosing my opposition XV, I have to admit that the selection is largely influenced by two matches. The first was the hardest I have played in. That was the game at Stade Colombes in 1971, when we won the Grand Slam. It was a ferocious 100 mph battle, with France having so many talented players – hard as nails – in key positions.

The other game was the humiliating defeat 19–0 against New Zealand in 1969. We were mere green pupils in a rugby classroom on that day. It was a trouncing, but our touring schedule did not help.

In the 1971 French game I came to appreciate the deceptive but thoughtful link play and flair of Pierre Villepreux. Always looking for attacking options, he was so comfortable with the ball. Little wonder that he went on to coach that flair at all levels, including the Italian national team. He was part of the French coaching team that won two Grand Slams and made a World Cup final appearance. Tracking him was a nightmare, and his positioning was sometimes so unorthodox that he was constantly popping up in support with superbly timed runs. And he was no mean kicker.

On the right wing is one of Gerald's best mates. If I wasn't playing, I loved watching David Duckham. He was a fair size, but once into his step, and blessed with that large sidestep which would evade your tackle, he was always dangerous. His centre partnership with John Spencer, before Carwyn James converted him to wing, was one of the most penetrative English partnerships. 'Dai', as he was crowned in Wales, was a very challenging customer, because as you chased across the field, you were ending your run when he was beginning his.

If John Dawes was our inspirational captain, there was

another player who mirrored John's analytical approach. Ironically, he was John's partner in the 1971 Lions team. Ireland's Mike Gibson was the complete footballer. He had pace, guile, vision and could split defensive patterns with the subtlest of body movement. If he thought you were in two minds, he'd be away.

Another centre to impress me was Jean-Pierre Lux. He won forty-seven caps for his country. He was deceptively quick, but also had changes of pace, which were always dangerous. You would plot an angle, and then suddenly you were confronted with an entirely different situation. He could play both centre and wing. An outstanding player, who went on to become chairman of the ERC.

My other wing will surprise many, since we did not see his best form in the union game. Keith Fielding became a dual union and league international. He was simply deceptive 'gas'. He was a tremendous athlete as well, as he proved during his stunning performances in *Superstars*.

The outside half factory was based in Wales, so it is fair to say that we were lucky to have the best in Barry and Phil. One opponent did catch my eye, and though he only won ten caps, I thought Micky Quinn of Ireland to be an exceptionally talented player. He was wily, without fuss, and with Mike Gibson outside him, it was a combination to watch and respect. Anyway, Micky once broke Walter Spanghero's nose with an outside half punch. Now that is noteworthy. I'd choose Micky, just shading it in front of Jo Maso of France – a real box of tricks.

The scrum half berth belongs to Sid Going. The first time I met him was on the 1969 tour, and even Gareth confesses he played second string that day. He had everything in the armoury. Running low, strong and stocky, he was not afraid of the contact area, and as a sniper he was an ideal scrum half to have behind that formidable All Black pack.

My front row is truly international. Ken Gray was an exceptionally strong Wellington farmer. He could play tight or loose, and had played lock as well. He was immense, and it was our misfortune to meet him in his last two games where he almost took us apart on his own. He played twenty-six Tests in total, and fifty in a black jersey. The All Blacks rate him as one of their best – enough said.

John Pullin of Bristol achieved legendary status when leading England to victories over South Africa, Australia and New Zealand, all in the space of eighteen months. He was a member of the 1971 Lions and played in that brilliant game for the Barbarians against the All Blacks. In total he won forty-two caps, a remarkable total for a hooker. Like Ken Gray, he was a farmer, naturally strong and extremely competitive.

Alongside John I would place his 1971 Lions partner, J. 'Mighty Mouse' McLauchlan. He was probably the best front row technician because, barrel-chested and small, he was able to burrow underneath his opponents and drive off the shove. He was everywhere in the loose, and the cornerstone of the Scotland and Lions scrum.

I have a confession to make when choosing my two locks. I did play against Colin Meads, who was a ferocious competitor, but I rated his brother Stan even more. He was a handful, and the toughest opponent I've met. I was in my first season with Neath and was selected to play for the Neath/Aberavon combined side against the All Black tourists. I couldn't believe his strength and power. We lost 11–6, but the memory of Stan Meads has stayed. He suffered badly from injuries, but when fit, he was as good as anyone. But in selecting a team, I haven't included either of the Meads.

Colin Meads reckons his toughest opponent was Walter Spanghero of France, and who am I to disagree with the All

Black legend. Spanghero could play just about anywhere – lock, number 8 or flanker. He had a massive jump, had pace around the park and could dominate a match like no one else I had seen. He was also a fair player. No nonsense, he just got on with what he was good at – dominating the line-out and broken play.

His partner would have to be Willie John McBride – heart of the Irish side, a member of the winning Lions in New Zealand and captain of the victorious Lions in South Africa. He was some competitor and motivator for all those around him. He also had presence. He was a huge competitor on the field and a good and honest man off it. Spanghero and McBride – that would be some combination.

So to the back row – those I have met so often on the gain line, face to face. In fact, this is my easiest task. At 6, I'd have Jean-Claude Skrela. What a player! A total poacher of any 50/50 ball. He was a brilliant pain! He was always in your face, and there was no surrender. His motivation was the same as mine – to go forward. He had a huge presence on the field. He had thought out his game, analysed what we or I would do, and there is no wonder that he eventually became one of the most successful of French coaches.

That coaching combination of him and Pierre Villepreux served France well. They were both inventive in their playing days as well as being instrumental in recapturing that flamboyant French flair as coaches. They were both born to attack, and they instilled that into the next generations.

I have no hesitation in my number 8 and 7. Both were immense, tough and inventive. I played against that fantastic South African back row of Greyling, Bedford and Ellis. They were tremendous as a unit. But for sheer power, drive and brilliance, I'd not seen better or more combative than Brian Lochore and Ian Kirkpatrick.

Ian Kirkpatrick was strong, resilient and quick. He carried

like a three-quarter, had the handling skills of an outside half, and a low shoulder charge that was difficult to challenge. Also he was everywhere, and had the battery to keep going until the final whistle. Great player – and later, as I found out, a great person.

It is strange that Brian Lochore, chosen as captain of the All Blacks, ahead of legendary names such as Meads, Tremain and Gray, always wanted to be a jockey. We had the love of horses in common, but on the field, he was a competitive but honest brute of a player. An all-time great All Black.

So that is my team – something to ponder upon and debate for the Rhigos RFC:

15. Pierre Villepreux (France)
14. David Duckham (England)
13. Jean Pierre Lux (France)
12. Mike Gibson (Ireland)
11. Keith Fielding (England)
10. Mike Quinn (Ireland)
9. Sid Going (New Zealand)
1. Ken Gray (New Zealand)
2. John Pullin (England)
3. 'Mighty Mouse' (Scotland)
4. Willy John McBride (Ireland)
5. Walter Spanghero (France)
6. Jean Claude Skrela (France)
7. Ian Kirkpatrick (New Zealand)
8. Brian Lochore (New Zealand) – captain

Now that game would have filled the Arms Park. But I don't think I'll go up the Rhigos Club for a while!

12

Lions 1971

OK, so I wasn't picked for the Lions 1971 tour to New Zealand, having been a member of that great Welsh side of 1971. Nothing to do with me! I had returned the invitation, by stating that I was available. There was outrage from Hirwaun to Glynneath, Neath and beyond because of my omission. There was a campaign in the *Western Mail*! Mervyn Davies and John Taylor were going, so should Dai. Why had I been singled out?

Could it be that I was too light to take on the All Blacks at the tail of the line-out, where they excelled? We had been physically hammered as a Welsh team in 1969 and that might have been a contributing factor. I heard all the arguments, and I don't think any of them hold any water.

I would have loved to take the All Blacks on – at their home! Why wasn't I picked? Just ask my great friend, Delme Thomas. He knew. Ask some of the other Welsh players – they also knew. Carwyn James, a selector and coach. I think he also knew and must have talked to Clive about that 1969 experience. Carwyn also had an up-and-coming uncapped flanker called Derek Quinnell is his back yard. And as history tells us Derek took his chance very well indeed.

Carwyn, especially, a great rugby brain, from a west Wales cultural environment, knew the weakness I had. I was too close to my community and family for a long three-month trip. I think he understood my dilemma. For the best part of fifty years I have driven home every night to Rhigos. Three months in New Zealand would probably have reduced me to an average rugby player, and in all probability a burden for the team management. I do get extremely homesick. In my mind, though, it is not a weakness, but a strength.

Though I had travelled to Australia, New Zealand, Fiji, Canada and Argentina by plane, I was never a comfortable passenger. I was a bag of nerves, if I'm honest. But all these had been relatively short tours. It is a well-known story that I had threatened some of the Welsh players with mortal damage on a propeller flight in New Zealand that if their drunken antics didn't stop and sway the plane one more time, I would deck them all, with some of them twice my size. The plane was moving in the wind, and they were creating havoc at the back. I was incensed, and they did take heed!

No, it wasn't air travel. It was just the length of the Lions tour. Delme went to South Africa with the Lions for five months – I couldn't believe that!

Don't think for a moment that I didn't want to go. There was a good representation from Wales, so that would have been OK. I would have known half the selected party. The NCB, especially the local chief in south Wales, Phillip Weekes, a keen rugby man, always saw to it that I didn't lose out financially if I was away with rugby.

I wasn't bitter. I just shrugged my shoulders and was content with twenty-six caps at that time. Not many people could claim that.

Lions 1971 was not to be. I could not be away from Rhigos for that length of time! And Carwyn knew it. Few people outside Rhigos know that I would have had to return from New Zealand, even if I had been selected.

A few weeks into the tour, my wife Marlene had a brain haemorrhage. It was serious, and she spent six weeks at Morriston Hospital receiving treatment and recovering. I was happy to be there for her.

There is more to life than rugby.

Tributes

Gareth Edwards CBE

I gave him the name 'Shadow', no matter what Clive Rowlands says. What you had from Dai, in every game, was a full shift. He would be everywhere. I can't remember him ever having a bad game, or doing anything wrong, and you cannot say that about many people.

His strength for one so slight was phenomenal, and if he got hold of you in opposition, then that was it. Those arms and claw hands were made of something special.

I think the hardest match he ever had was during that infamous round-the-world trip in 1969. We'd already been hammered by the All Blacks, beaten Australia, with Dai outstanding in that match and scoring a try, but then came Fiji.

It was meant to be a sort of development game to help Fiji raise funds. For 'development' read 'demolition'. Dai confessed to being battered and bruised by those big Fijian tacklers. He could hardly walk after that game. They threw their bodies at us, as if this was the last Fijian game for ever.

There was a hard sincerity to his game. Of course he had a feel for where he should be, and was invariably there in the right place where he was required. Except, on one occasion.

There have been countless replays of the try I scored against Scotland, with me ending up diving in the Arms Park 'red mud'. The try came at a stage of the match when Scotland had been playing well, and we needed to get back on terms with them. But if you take a closer look at the start of that movement, I had been given the ball by Mervyn Davies and gone past Roger Arneil, and I am looking left and right for support.

Where was he?

Normally Dai would be there, but he wasn't. He'd been drawn into a maul. So I had no option but to kick, chase, hack on and go for the corner. I keep saying in public that I scored that try, because Dai let me down!

But what a player! I can't praise him enough. The more I played with him, the more I respected him.

That back row of Dai, Mervyn Davies and John Taylor was one of the finest ever. They could adapt – and they were quick. Of its era, it was the most potent back row combination in rugby.

Ironically, it was a combination brought together because of a change in the law which allowed a four-man line-out. England used this against us with much taller locks and back row men. Mervyn was brought into the Welsh side by Clive for his height, and the other two were used as fast, low ground missiles.

It worked, but in that combination we had a tireless competitor in Dai. He was totally switched on, but not on tour. He was fine on the field, but off, his mind was in Rhigos. We were constantly told what was happening in Rhigos since he refused to change his watch.

He knew everything about what was going on back home. He knew everyone's routine, and all he wanted to know was how Helen his young daughter was coping. He could tell you what each farmer was doing in Rhigos, or what shifts the miners were on.

It was just like listening to 'First Voice' in *Under Milk Wood*. He was very much a home bird and perhaps that is why he didn't join us in New Zealand in 1971. He should have.

Gerald Davies CBE

He was a 'shadow' on the field, and was invisible elsewhere. In changing rooms, hotels or in company, Dai was hardly ever heard. But, if he did say something it was invariably worth listening to.

I can still see him now on the morning of an international. He'd be immaculately dressed, complete with his favourite Barbarian tie, and you'd swear he hadn't been to bed. Most of us would be in tracksuits, T-shirts and shorts. Dai could have presented himself to Buck House – he was that smart. Sadly, he did not receive that recognition. Delme, his constant companion, was also quite dapper in the morning, along with John Lloyd.

He was a true Corinthian who firmly believed in the spirit and ethos of the game. There was no nonsense about him, and I can't say that about some of his colleagues at the Gnoll.

Dai let his rugby do the talking, and the fact that he scored so many tries for Neath, Glynneath and Wales shows that he was always on hand, and never far behind the ball carrier.

He was one of the most sincere of players, but I cannot recall a single discussion with him about any game. He played the game and that was it. There was little chat.

There wasn't much of him. Just bone and hard muscle. One thing we did share in common: we were the only two in that Welsh team with twenty-eight-inch waists. Me, as a 5' 8½" centre or winger, and Dai a 6' 13 st. number 8 or 6.

He was so quiet, I don't recall his first appearance against France in Paris. Apparently, he slipped into the Hotel Normandie, having travelled there by the Dover/Calais ferry, and returned by the same route. That is him – the invisible shadow.

It was also Gareth's first cap as a ravenous 19-year-old student. He made his first appearance memorable by eating two steak and chip lunches before going on to play a blinder against the French. Naturally we did not have dieticians with us in those days.

Dai was not a comfortable tourist. On the field he was fine, but in between games, he was not happy to be away from his familiar territory of Rhigos. No man has loved that area more than Dai.

I don't know, but I suspect that his *hiraeth* for home was the reason he was not selected for the 1971 Lions. It certainly wasn't for his playing ability.

John Dawes OBE
Captain and coach of Wales and British Lions

I think Dai's omission from the Lions 1971 party was down to a number of factors. We were, collectively, as Welsh players on that tour desperately disappointed that he was not chosen.

I think Carwyn James, who obviously had a major influence on selection, had taken heed of the Welsh experience during the 1969 New Zealand tour. New Zealand had been particularly strong at the back of the line-out, and had some major players there like Ian Kirkpatrick. Mervyn and John were not bulky back row men, and having someone there to block the All Black drive was a major issue. This was the area where Carwyn thought that New Zealand would attack us – and they did. It wasn't the fact that Dai wasn't good enough – he wasn't big enough.

He would also have been aware, through Clive Rowlands, that Dai had been uncomfortable during that 1969 tour. It wasn't only the length of it – it was all the hours spent flying – and Dai wasn't a good passenger.

But, principally, I think it was a technical decision. The uncapped Derek Quinnell was chosen for a purpose – to stop the inevitable drive from the set pieces.

Here at home, I think for many reasons, Dai's name would have been the first to go down on the Welsh team list.

Dai was always there, perpetual motion, always consistent. If you asked me what he did: did he throw a dummy? Did he kick? Or did he do something extraordinary? The answer would be 'No'. He was known for always being there.

I can't remember ever talking to him on the pitch, or even before or after a game. But he was Mr Reliable. If there was a mistake, he didn't have the John Taylor glare which we all experienced at some time, Dai would just carry on.

But for a quiet man, he thoroughly enjoyed the company of others. He joined in everything, but you wouldn't want to ask Dai to give a solo. That would have frightened him stiff!

Barry John
British Lions and Wales

If you go up to the Rhigos Rugby Club, there's a board there which lists all the guest speakers they've had for various functions. It's a 'who's who' of the rugby world. I was completely overawed by it, but then I shouldn't have been surprised. It just demonstrated the respect everyone has had for Dai – a man of few words but massive integrity.

On the field, if I went on one of my running jaunts and suddenly felt the whole world closing in on me, all I had to do and did was pop up the ball over my head, because I knew that the ever present W.D. Morris would be there.

I do remember challenging him to a race at a Llanrumney training session.

"Come on, Dai. On the count of three."

Naturally I went on two, just to get ahead of him.

He passed me like a thoroughbred, and clipped me on the ear. Beaten by a back row man!

The thing is, when we got back to the changing room, he hadn't told a soul.

John Taylor

London Welsh, Wales and British Lions

There were those who cast us as 'chalk and cheese'. Some intentionally put forward the theory that as two flankers we didn't or couldn't get along, because he was the local lad from Rhigos and I was this boy down from London. Some did try to drive a rift between us. But nothing could be further from the truth. We got on superbly well. All three of us in the back row, Dai, Mervyn and I.

On the field the working relationship was perfect. We understood each other and, what many people tend to overlook, we were able to do what we did because of Mervyn's dominance at the tail of the line-out and the control at the back of the scrum. We were allowed to be free agents.

He wasn't a happy tourist, and being away from home did affect his game. That was particularly true of the 1969 Welsh tour to New Zealand, Australia and Fiji. He went into his shell a bit.

I also recall him giving me a right telling off in Canada. I think I was the pack leader and we were in the middle of a training session in Edmonton. We were going through various moves, patterns, individual responsibilities and calls. Then Dai erupted, "Why are you making the game so bloody complicated?"

Many years after finishing our playing careers we were at a function in Pontarddulais. It was here that he told me that his true playing weight all those years ago was never over 13 stone. I couldn't believe it, because personally I was having a go at John Reason of the *Telegraph* who did the international programme profiles that my weight was always printed as being 13 st. 7 1b, though in fact I was 14 st. and had worked at it in the gym. It annoyed me that Reason would not believe me. I had no idea that during all those years we played together and against each other, Dai had been a stone lighter.

I didn't mind playing against him for London Welsh. It was always a tough but fair competition. But in the south Wales clubs in those days you had the likes of Morrie Evans at Swansea, Omri Jones at Aberavon, Hickey at Cardiff – they were different. At least with Dai it was always a competitive battle for supremacy. He wasn't on the field to kick ten bells out of you.

But I did have occasion to give him a telling off. Pat Collins, the respected *Mail on Sunday* journalist, wanted to feature a Welsh player, and had sought my advice. He was keen to do a profile of Denzil Williams, but I thought that he might get a better story if he travelled to Rhigos to do a piece on Dai. Pat loved the experience and could not praise Dai enough.

On his return, he thanked me for the tip and told me that Dai would have liked me to be a guest speaker at their annual dinner, but was too shy to ask. I rang Dai up, and gave him a right bollocking for not asking me, and of course I would be there. What a night at the Baverstock Hotel on the heads of the valleys road.

Almost as memorable, but for entirely different reasons, was the one time I saw Dai a bit the worse for wear. It was Paris in 1969, and we had drawn our match against a strong French side in their back yard. Celebrations were in order, since the draw meant we had won the championship. There were drinks after the game, drinks back at Hotel Normandie and at the official reception every table was stacked with bottles of wine. Everywhere we went, there was wine.

The lot of them were going for it, apart from Gerald and myself, since we'd been there before, and knew what was coming. Then, back at the hotel, Denzil Williams suggested a game of French 'buzz'. Dai and Delme couldn't cope with French numerals, and were heavily and constantly penalised. Suddenly Dai didn't feel too well, and left. After a while a search party went looking for him, including myself and John Lloyd.

We found him in the gents, leaning over the toilet bowl, but with his hands in the water. He really was in an agitated state, and we tried to pull him up and away. He turned around and gave Bev Price, the captain, a smack in the chops for his good intentions.

Dai had been ill, but had also lost his teeth in the bowl, and was desperately trying to retrieve them.

Dai Davies
Neath, Swansea and Dai's 'best man'

There are only a few things I remember about Dai and Marlene's wedding. It seemed short, quick and quiet – no nonsense – get it over with and go!

It was held at Penderyn Church in one of the remotest parts of the Brecon Beacons. Those who have been to Ystradfellte will know what I mean. Perfect for Dai, since no one else would be around.

He'd asked the rector for a morning service so that he could play in the afternoon. The vicar said no. Wedding kick-off 2.00 p.m! So Dai's main concern at the reception in the Black Lion in Aberdare was that we were both missing a Neath game at Ebbw Vale, and that we might be dropped because of our absence. He always has been a worrier. I know he played for Neath after his sister's morning wedding.

Dai and Marlene had been courting for a while. When I say 'courting' it would involve picking Marlene up in Resolven, where she was a hairdresser, and then driving down to a training session at the Gnoll. He'd leave Marlene at my house in King Street with my Joan, and then pick her up after training for the drive home. Romantic? He couldn't spell it.

I was the players' representative when Dai arrived at

Neath. John Davies, a super number 8, had gone north, and Dai had come down from that impressive Glynneath team.

Being a players' representative meant looking after the welfare of the boys, but it was a struggle with a nineteen-strong committee. They were an awkward bloody-minded bunch of so-and-sos to say the least.

Initially, the players were given five shillings a game – which could buy you a few pints. But you didn't have to be a mathematician to work out that with packed houses at the Gnoll, with a gate charge of 1s 3d (13p), somebody was making money. It certainly wasn't the players. I negotiated a rise to 10s a game (50p) – a fortune, even though they argued that they had a player's maximum fee agreement with other first-class clubs in the area. A claim that was totally untrue.

He's one of the most unassuming guys ever. He could be riled though. I remember a county game between Glamorgan and Monmouthshire at Newport and his opposite number was Derek Brain. I don't know what was going on, but Dai was bothered. It must have been some niggly jersey pulling. But Dai said to me, "I am going to give him one if he doesn't stop."

"You're going to give him one?" I asked, because, from Dai, this was unheard of. Anyway, in a few minutes, Derek got up off the floor and his eye was like a balloon. Dai said nothing, just carried on, but that was the only time I remember him on the dark side of the game, a place where I was often known to frequent.

Dai and I were, and still are, close friends. Dai would insist that we drive to all the away games. He never wanted to go on the team bus, and I know why. The team bus wouldn't stop at a bookie, would it! He didn't gamble that much, he just had an immense fascination, and indeed knowledge, about the racing industry. So inevitably we would be the last to arrive at the changing rooms of south Wales, but at least we could avoid the pre-match 'meditation' sessions conducted by Grahame Hodgson. 'Meditation at Neath' – I ask you!

That Neath side was formidable in every sense. Randall, my brother, relished the physical confrontations. There was one notorious game against Cardiff in 1967. It was the second game of the season, and Cardiff were always a priority target for Neath.

It was ill-tempered and Randall was in the middle of most of it. His battle with Denis Hickey was raw to say the least, and Randall was sent off and subsequently banned for three months by the WRU. We were due to go to London Welsh for our next game, but the players were so incensed by the ban that they said they wouldn't travel. Rees Stephens, a Neath, Wales and Lions legend and also a Welsh selector, stepped in, and said that if we didn't travel, not one of us would play for Wales or play Welsh club rugby ever again! Just imagine if we had stuck to our guns. Dai hadn't been capped then. But games between the two clubs were suspended for four years. It was that bad!

Then I had one row too many with the Neath committee. They didn't select me for one game in order to have a look at a new recruit from Maesteg. I was furious, since we had an agreed rota system between Brian Thomas, Barry Thomas and myself. So I left Neath to join Swansea – I was that fed up with the committee.

I shall never forget my first game for Swansea against Neath and my former mates. I caught a high ball from a kick-off, and I was smashed to the floor, writhing in pain with two cracked ribs. The tacklers were my brother Randall and the groom of Ystradfellte, Dai Morris!

Glyn Shaw
Neath, Wales and Widnes

Though I was born in Rhigos, the first time I met Dai was in the Neath changing room. I'd been snapped up by Neath after a few games with Seven Sisters Rugby Club. I'm told I was spotted by Brian Thomas and Ron Waldron heaving weights and trams at the colliery.

We became firm friends from that moment. We eventually became workmates at Tower – I was underground, Dai was upstairs.

We travelled together to all the games, and that was the most frightening part of the day. Dai was always late, and always the driver. He would leave everything to the last minute, and then drive down to Neath like a bat out of hell.

Tom Lewis and Dai Pumps would come with us sometimes as well, and I can't count the number of times he would jump out of the car outside the Gnoll, with the engine still running and ask the boys to park it somewhere. Both of us would have to make a dash for the changing room.

If Neath, and then the WRU, had allowed him to change into his kit at home, and then travel to the Gnoll or Cardiff, he would have been happy. He just hated any changing room and waiting around to get onto the field.

Even on international days, he'd take me around the corner to find a bookie, and we would stay there to listen for 'just one more race' before walking down to the Arms Park where the rest of the players were already in their kit and Welsh jerseys. He didn't bet that much, it was just a distraction.

In many ways we were alike. I couldn't eat on match days. Nothing was right before a match – I'd worry about the game, my aches and pains, and I would be physically sick with nerves. Absolutely terrible. Then you went onto the field, and wait for the kick-off. Suddenly everything vanished. There were no doubts then, because you had a job to do. Everything became clear, and it was a great feeling of release.

Dai, I think, was like that as well. He was a greyhound in a trap, but once the game was underway, he didn't stop running, and he would do his job. He would try and do everybody else's job as well. At times he was a bloody nuisance, and you had to tell him. He was the perfect flanker in that era of the game.

And during that time we befriended Wayne Cornelius, who was wheelchair-bound and suffered from speech and physical disabilities. Dai and I took him in the car from Rhigos to the Gnoll, even to training nights, and to internationals for several years, always finding him the best place in the house. He didn't complain about Dai's driving either. After a game I used to wind Wayne up by telling him that Dai had played a bad one, and that would set Wayne off. Though he had a speech impediment, I knew exactly what he was telling me. To Wayne, Dai was God!

Grahame Hodgson
Wales and Neath

David's strength-to-weight ratio was astonishing. He was so strong, thin and muscular but if he tackled you in training, then you appreciated what he did to the opposition in a game. He was also very quick, with an amazing stride. He could ride tackles with ease, and if your tackle wasn't totally sound he was away, in only one direction – forward. I am not sure whether he was a great reader of a game, because he didn't have to be, since wherever the ball was, David was not far away.

We had a few hard players at Neath who would and could mix it in dark places, but never David. He had this very strong belief in fair play.

He always brought a quiet enthusiasm to the team, because

there was nothing he enjoyed more than going forward and creating momentum. As a unit, he, Wilson Lauder, Alan Butler or Mike Thomas had the ability to adjust. Like all good back row forwards, he would sweep up at the breakdown, and continue the movement. He'd carry and carry, ride those tackles, all at speed.

He was not of the teaching manual, that's for sure. He didn't like my coaching lessons, and once walked off. Anyway, what Dai had, you couldn't teach.

I'm sure Dai Parker will also vouch that he was the 'great protector' of the ball, and woe betide anyone who gave Dai Parker a hard time. To David it was all about doing the business – his business.

Dai Watkins MBE
Wales, Newport and Salford

I only played twice with Dai for Wales. Barry John had played a couple of times in the number 10 jersey, but then I was brought back as captain against France and England in 1967.

My recollection of the young Dai Morris was his appetite for the game. He was always fair, but had that presence about him. He seemed to be running all the time, and never more than a couple of yards from the ball.

I suppose I saw more of Dai in opposition. Neath was a difficult place to go, not nice at all. We'd shut the changing room windows so as not to hear that black Gnoll crowd. They were something else! I know that Alan Dix, their open-side flanker at the time, used to frighten me stiff.

Neath had two Cambridge graduates in the pack, Roger Michaelson and Brian Thomas, but you soon realised that there was nothing academic about their approach to the game.

That Neath pack was a handful. If you made a break, you

might have beaten the first man, but the second opponent would invariably be Dai. He rarely missed a tackle. It was always hard but fair, which is more than I can say about some of the other Neath characters. The battles between Brian Price and Brian Thomas, who became the closest of friends, were not for the weak hearted. Add the likes of the Davies boys, Wilson Lauder, Ron Waldron – no wonder I went north.

Ron Waldron
Wales and Neath player and coach

He only had one direction, and that was forward. There was nothing lateral about Dai. Some of our training sessions were much harder than the games, especially if you had the likes of Dai and Glyn Shaw roaming around.

I have only seen one modern player who remotely compares with the energy and commitment shown by Dai Morris – and that is Sam Warburton. But Dai was only just over 13 st. in wet socks.

He was also brought up in a side that believed if a flanker was beaten for pace by a half back, they'd be mortified. Dai had pace all right, but he also had a mental hardness to go with it.

He had this instinct of being in the right place at the right time – a great link man in attack, and his work rate in defence was uncompromising. It was the same in every game, whether it was for Neath, Wales or his beloved Rhigos. He just wanted to play – and he played at the same pace and ferocity from beginning to end. He had this mentality of being totally focused on what had to be done. He could just switch it on. And I can't remember him saying anything on the field. Just an amazing player – up there with the best that Wales has produced.

I remember going up to Tower Colliery with some of the Neath players and some French visitors, with Dai showing us around. When you saw his workplace, the conditions underground and the machinery and tools they lifted all day, you realised how hard these men were – Dai and Glyn Shaw. Brian Thomas was with us, one of the most feared of Welsh locks, but even he was reduced to a whimpering mess at the thought of going down in the colliery cage. Dai just smiled.

And don't forget, both Dai and Glyn were known to have worked shifts before driving down to the Gnoll for an evening game. Incredible!

Delme Thomas
British Lions, Wales and Llanelli

He was one of the hardest men ever in a Welsh jersey, but always a gentleman. That was Dai. To be tackled by Dai was like being confronted by a motor bike travelling at 50 miles an hour. He was so hard, uncompromising, but always fair. Yet every bone in your body felt a Dai tackle! And if he was hurt, he never showed it. You could see that sometimes he was in pain – but there was no surrender. I can't recall a trainer being called onto the field to treat him.

He was also one of the fittest people I have played with or against. Dai was fit in pre-season, when the rest of us were struggling a bit. And he lived for his rugby.

Once the game was over that was it. He didn't want to talk about it, or analyse everything, as modern pundits do. He'd rather talk about anything but rugby – and you'd have his undivided attention if you talked about horses. I enjoyed his company.

Wherever we were, Dai's first question would be to enquire about the nearest stables. Even in Canada he sought out the mountain police and their stables – and John Lloyd and I went with him!

He didn't particularly like the post-match international

official dinners, and once it was deemed polite to leave, he would, with John Lloyd and me in tow. Then we'd meet up with Tom Lewis and Dai Pumps, his best mates from Rhigos, in a nearby hotel. He wasn't comfortable with all the fans around either, especially in Cardiff, so we'd find a little corner in the Angel Hotel or the Model Inn and talk about everything apart from rugby. He was at his best if the chat was a good laugh. He'd really enjoy that!

The other chat he would enjoy was with Clive Rowlands, the Welsh coach. There was huge mutual respect as their backgrounds were pretty similar. Clive had the ability to bring out the best in Dai. He was almost an adopted son to Clive. Clive expected a performance from Dai – and in truth Dai never let him down. Dai didn't have an ego either – and that appealed to Clive.

I did see him lose it once. I think it was in Canada. Dai trod on some glass in a hotel swimming pool, and cut himself badly. The late John Billot, a *Western Mail* journalist, somehow got to hear about this, and the next morning there was a headline in Wales about the 'Dai Morris injury'. Dai heard about this report, and he was so incensed that some of us feared for John Billot's welfare and future. Throughout his career Dai was never 'injured'. He played on regardless.

But he did render us helpless with laughter. Clive had gone to bed one morning with flu and had asked John Taylor to take the forwards session. Now John was a real talker, big long words, with a Watford accent. The longer the session went on, the more agitated Dai became.

After a while Dai had enough, and shouted "For Christ sake, John, come down a step, we need a dictionary to understand you!" End of session! Total collapse of the squad and the session!

John Lloyd
Bridgend, Wales captain and coach

He was unbelievably strong. His fitness was incredible, hard manual labour at the colliery for eight hours a day – lifting rings, hammering away, plus training – he rarely stopped. If you were playing against him, you'd never get the ball off him. I prided myself on being a good mauler – but you rarely got the better of Dai. That unit of Dai, Mervyn Davies and John Taylor was telepathic, because I can't remember them talking. They communicated somehow, and always worked together to win games. It was the cornerstone of the Welsh side – not the front row!

He also had what I would call a sixth sense – a great rugby brain – knowing exactly where to be at the breakdown. Following the ball was his forte – I don't know how many miles he'd run during a game, but he always seemed to be there – especially behind Gareth.

We became great friends and, together with Delme, became a small group that enjoyed each other's company – talking and socialising. He was shy, there's no denying that, but on the morning of a match in Cardiff, Edinburgh or Dublin, he'd be the first up, dressed and off to a nearby bookie. He loved his horses, and then at the end of a game, he'd find out the results, and off he went scurrying to the bookie through the crowds to check the results, and possibly collect some winnings!

Not many of the Welsh players enjoyed the tour to Argentina. We were housed in a country club in the middle of the country. Phil Bennett enjoyed his snooker, Clive Rowlands enjoyed going to Patagonia, but if you didn't play golf or squash – there was nothing else to do. I have to admit that I enjoyed the steaks! But for Dai, it was a great tour. The country club had horses, gauchos, stables – and

Dai was in his element. And could he handle those horses! The gauchos had huge hands – but so did Dai.

But one day a horse broke its leg, and they killed it on the spot with a knife to the heart, blood pouring everywhere. Dai was mortified.

He hated flying. I can remember him totally losing it on one flight when the big brutes at the back were having a major liquid session and matters were getting out of order. It wasn't a big plane, one of those prop jobs you only see in films. If the boys at the back were in full swing, so was the plane. As they rocked and jumped at the back so too did the plane. Dai couldn't stand it anymore and physically threatened the lot of them – if they didn't sit down he'd smash them. They sat down. Even in their liquefied state, they had respect for Dai. But he was never comfortable on a plane, and on the request of Clive Rowlands, Dai and I would regularly leave a day early for Edinburgh or Dublin by boat and train.

Phil Bennett OBE
British Lions, Wales and Llanelli captain

I can honestly say that Dai Morris probably saved my life. It was a match at the Gnoll, and Llanelli had taken a very depleted side there, on a grim wet Wednesday night, which was suicidal to say the least. Our 'old heads' weren't there, and I was made captain.

We were getting hammered – Scarlet lambs to the Welsh All Black slaughterers. Then I fell on a loose ball, and the Neath pack were trundling towards me. Suddenly from nowhere, there is Dai falling on top of me and telling me to stay down. He took a 'shoeing' for me, for which I and my family are very grateful.

I know that others will recall his endurance, fitness and non-stop activity on the field. I think he is one of the most loyal of people.

Long after we had retired from international and first-class rugby, both of us would be involved in invitational internationals teams with matches to celebrate an event, a clubhouse opening or lights being installed.

Invariably, you'd enter the clubhouse or changing room, and Dai would be there. I don't think he could refuse.

We had a celebration game at my home club in Felinfoel, and I had the task of raising the invitation XV. Dai had been invited and turned up. He hadn't bothered to tell me he was injured, and he played the full game with a serious limp. Hell of a man and friend.

I also remember Bobby Windsor taking a team to Mountain Ash. I am not sure to this day whether Bobby was paid a fee for organising the invitational XV, but there was me, Bobby and the rest were Pontypool United players – and Mountain Ash were no slouches.

When we took to the field, I recognised one familiar face in the Mountain Ash team. One Dai Morris! What the hell was he doing there? I knew that I was in for a busy night, because there was one thing about Dai – Wales, Neath, Glynneath, Rhigos or Mountain Ash – he'd never stop.

If you had to raise a team, Dai would be there for you.

Dai Parker
Neath and Swansea

There was nothing you could dislike about Dai. I didn't know him that well when I first joined Neath. The late Martyn Davies was the Neath scrum half – and a very good one too. So we shared the position, or I would play outside half. Then Martyn went off to play for Cardiff College of Further Education. So, as the Neath scrum half, I very quickly appreciated the talents of Dai Morris.

He was the ideal number 8. He would never deliver bad ball, and gave you Fort Knox protection. His support play was exceptional, and if someone was giving me some bother, Dai would sort it out. He'd follow the action everywhere.

I can remember our winger Elgan Rees setting off on one of his famous zigzag jinking runs. No one knew where Elgan was heading, least of all himself. The rest of us just watched. But not Dai. He was there to receive the scoring pass after trailing Elgan for about 70 yards.

He was immense, and a firm believer in fair play. He couldn't stand rough or dirty nonsense, and if he did see something he didn't like, especially by the opposition – then look out. "Don't touch the ball" he would shout at a ruck, "Don't touch the ball!" Then, he'd pick up the ball and charge at the culprit with all his might. The sight of Dai in full flight deliberately looking for contact was something else. I remember him doing it against Aberavon, when someone had broken Barry Davies's jaw. He took the ball and ran towards the Aberavon pack. They didn't want to know.

And yet it would never be beyond the law – just hard – and the one on the receiving end would get the message. Because of my size he was particularly protective of me, and when I'd been kicked by an Argentinian tourist in a match, Dai chased him all over the field. He was not someone to mess around.

He was too shy to be a captain, but he was a leader, and his greatest pleasure, apart from the horses, was to play the game. He could pout though. There was one occasion when Dai had played for Wales at Twickenham on the Saturday, but then turned up on the following Monday night at Cross Keys expecting to play. He was not best pleased to hear that he hadn't been selected. Words were exchanged – somebody had to stand down – and Dai played.

It was after our playing days had finished that we became close friends. Dai would be invited to countless functions to say a few words. That is the problem. Dai is a man of few words – so he would take me along as a deputy speaker since I am not a man of 'a few words'.

His passion for his home village of Rhigos and the family is only matched by his passion for horses. I like a bet myself, not quite as much as Dai, but his knowledge of the turf is immense, and I suspect that his zest for owning and training has cost him a small fortune. One thing is for certain – if it has, he won't tell you how much!

I was told a story about one of Dai's horses. It can't be true – or can it? This horse of Dai's was so bad that on a homeward journey Dai, Tom and Dai Pumps considered abandoning it on the Severn Bridge.

It may have been Dai Pumps who said "We could leave him here now, and run away from him. He won't catch us!"

Vince Good
Glynneath

That early period in Glynneath was as good as it gets. We had a fine combination of seasoned players, and very good young ones coming through. Most were colliers. Hard, uncompromising, mean.

Some were exceptionally talented. David Weaver, a future international, was one, together with Neath players from the past and for the future in Lyn Tregonning, Johnny Weaver, Graham Prosser and Dai Owen.

I remember Dai's first try – he was seventeen, having just come up from youth.

That run of fifty-five games without defeat was memorable. So too were the club tours to Penzance and Falmouth. The least said about those the better, since there are some hoteliers in the West Country still looking for their furniture.

The Late Peter Davies
Neath and Wigan

I remember the first time I met Dai. I'd been picked for the Glamorgan side to play North Wales in Bangor. I was playing for Neath at the time, but the bus on its way north picked up four boys from the successful side at Glynneath – and Dai was one of them. He got on the bus, never said a word and went to the back to play cards.

Next thing I knew, Dai was packing down with me in the second row. I couldn't believe that this string bean, weighing 13 st., had been picked in the engine room. I could almost lift him with one arm. But he was rock hard.

He had the last laugh. He scored four tries in that game, two of them 60-yard runs. Now I couldn't do that.

He came up with me to Wigan. I had joined as a professional, and we were playing Castleford. Dai went off to play for the Wigan A team against St Helens. He was voted man of the match, and was paid a £50 fee and £14 travelling expenses. So he bought an engagement ring for Marlene.

He was not only an astonishing player, but a remarkable person.

There were several players in those days who had a 'side' to them. Not Dai. He was always true.

Glen Ball
Neath and Wales tour to Argentina

I have never seen anything like him. He was non-stop. There was no waste in his play, whether it was in support, linking, tackling and protecting. He was ideal for me as a centre, since I knew he would be there at any breakdown.

You come across a few players like that – they have this sixth sense of what is going to happen and when.

Not many sides relished the prospect of facing the Neath

pack in those days. We did have a few rough diamonds, and some of the things going on would make you wince. As a back, you could see it all. But Dai was never part of that.

Of course he was always the last to arrive in the changing room, always missing the team talk – and then straight out on the field. But we put up with that, because he was special.

And I can't remember if I ever heard him talk on the field either!

Clive Harris and Graham Lewis
Rhigos treasurer and secretary

Dai was very much the inspiration behind the reforming of the Rhigos club. He became coach, captain, chief selector and bus driver.

He didn't have to. He was a Wales player, Neath RFC stalwart, and had played against the best in the world. But he wanted a Rhigos team.

The selection committee met in the back room of the Plough Inn, all twenty-one of them, and the meetings would last for hours. Trevor 'The Plough' would eventually have to chuck them out.

The Plough was our HQ, but we played at the Welfare Ground in Glynneath, since we didn't have our own ground until a few years later.

When we started, it was the first time some of the boys had played rugby, but we were joined by Rhigos players who had experience from surrounding clubs.

That first season was the only time we saw Dai train. A two-and-a-half-mile run around the village, with intermittent squats – a real killer for us, but a stroll for him. During games he would pace himself, just above the rest of us. But he did have an incredible memory for faces, and if he recognised an ex-first-class player in the opposition, then he would go up a few gears. That was all about pride – but we couldn't match that pace.

And he was a stickler for fair play. If he saw one of our boys do something dirty, he would tell them straight away "Do that one more time, and you will never play for Rhigos again". If the opposition did something to one of our boys, then Dai would call for the ball and run straight at the culprit – and the matter would be resolved.

His greatest moment in a Rhigos jersey was when he played alongside his son Greg in the back row. Greg was a very useful young player, still in youth, when they first played together. That probably gave Dai more satisfaction than a Welsh cap.

Graham would organise the annual dinner and bash. It was quite a lavish do. Four buses from Rhigos, leaving the village empty as we headed every year to the Seabank Hotel in Porthcawl.

Now Dai did enjoy a drop of whisky, and we all remember one incident. The man in charge of the four buses said he was leaving Porthcawl at midnight, but Graham had booked a 1.30 a.m. departure, after the dinner.

The driver was having none of it, and in stepped Dai. He caught hold of the driver by the throat, until he turned blue and told the driver "If Graham says he wants to leave at 1.30, we will leave at 1.30! OK?"

We left at 1.30 a.m., and Dai was happy.

Dai Walters
Dai's employer, Rhigos-born chairman of the Walters Group of Companies, and the owner of Ffos Las Racecourse

A more loyal and conscientious man I can't imagine. He's been here at the Follies, my home and racing yard in Cardiff for some fifteen years.

This means he's travelled from Rhigos, where we were both born and brought up, at 6.30 a.m. in the morning, and hasn't left, at times, until seven in the evening. It is a round trip of some fifty miles. He is tireless, and I know that what drives him on is his passion for working with horses – and all animals – but more of that later.

I have had to cut down his hours, with a few sharp words, because I was concerned about his health. He still travels early, but goes home at lunchtime, and he doesn't come on Sundays. He's moaned about the new agreement, but I've cut his hours for his own good.

As a youngster in Rhigos I was closer to Colin his brother. Rhigos was not a large village, but it was a very happy one, with everybody knowing everybody else – and their business. Colin and I were the same age, Dai was a little older.

But it is his passion for animals that has continually amazed us at the Hollies in Lisvane. He cannot abide any animal being harmed. He rescued a mouse in a stables trap and then let it loose – bloody hell! We'd put the trap down because the mouse was attacking feed bags. But there was one incident which has become folklore for us.

It was winter, and our pond was frozen solid and our ducks had taken refuge on the island pond. There was one very large duck, and a neighbourhood fox had taken a liking to the ducks.

The fox got across the ice and had a go at the ducks, killing two or three of them but the largest duck was probably too big a prey. But severe damage was done.

Enter Dai Morris, clambering over the ice and rescuing the duck, and over a few weeks, nurtured it back to full health with milk bottles, and placing it with the fenced chickens for company.

A few weeks on, Dai would arrive at work, whistle, and the large duck would follow him around! We now have the largest duck in Wales – completely protected by Dai. Absolutely amazing! He has always had an affinity with animals that I have not seen before.

It was his strength – but also his weakness. I will leave him to tell the story of his triumphs with his horse, Helen's Vision.

But, like his rugby, you will always get 100 per cent. If I go away on business, I can always count on Dai to give me a briefing on my return of what has been going on, and what needs to be done. And it is always down to the finest detail.

One thing he can't do is remember where he's left his tools. There's a fortune of tools lying around the yard somewhere. A terrible memory, but a great friend.

Helen Morris
Daughter

It was a fantastic childhood, since everything was to do with animals and the outdoors. We spent most of the time over at Tom's farms, who also bought me a pony when I was two. I'd spend hours and days over there, riding, helping with the animals, haymaking – and I know that my son Joseph is infatuated with animals too and has inherited that from being around one of the most obsessed animal-loving families ever.

Yes, I am as soft as my father. I've still got a stray dog, fifteen years after it was abandoned, together with a collie from Tom's farm and, yes, I will confess that I went to a supermarket to buy biscuits to feed some ragged-looking valley sheep.

I also love horse racing, and I can remember my first introduction. I was told, as a young girl, to stay outside as my father went into the Rhigos bookie. I never went in, but I can still remember the radio commentaries. I spent a lot of time outside the bookies.

Of course, when we all went to the Ascot sales, with Greg in the pram, and bought Princess Glory, this was a new dimension. I loved it all.

I knew my father had played for Wales but I wasn't aware at that age what it all meant. My mother tells me that I was taken to one international match, and slept right through it. She also tells me, because I don't remember these things, that the only thing I enjoyed that weekend was going up and down in the Angel Hotel lift.

I have never seen him angry. I have never heard him swear. He was mending a car outside the house, and it was proving to be a difficult job. So he asked my mother to go inside, just in case he said something she would not want to hear. That is him.

We had a great childhood.

Greg Morris
Son

I played with my father in the Rhigos team, some eight or nine times, since invariably Rhigos were always one short in the pack – and you know exactly who would volunteer to make up the numbers.

I was also there when he cracked his ribs in the last game for Rhigos, when he had promised my mother he would never play again.

Perhaps I could have made the grade at first-class level, since I had played for the Neath district at youth level, and had been selected for a Welsh youth trial. On the eve of the trial, I was involved in a motor accident and couldn't play. I know that was a huge disappointment for Dad.

However, I was invited to join the Brive under-21 academy in France, but their promises of work and contracts came to nothing, so back I came after a month.

I did find it hard being the son of Dai Morris. Wherever we

went, he, quite naturally, was the centre of attention. I felt, as a player and as a person, that I was always being measured up against him. I was uncomfortable with that. That doesn't mean I resented his fame, I just wanted to be myself.

Dai Pumps, one of the family's great friends, reckoned I had more potential than Dad, and I would like to see his reaction when he reads that.

When he's watched me play, he'll tell me what I haven't done. He's like that with the kids even now. He is always telling you what they could do better.

Outside rugby, both my parents have been immense. Not only to me, Helen and the kids, but the community around us. He will do anyone a favour if he can.

Yes, I, too, have been indoctrinated into Morris animal husbandry and care addiction. We currently have Winne and Agnes, two pet lambs, and about two dozen chickens and one cockerel.

I also went one step further than Helen. Dad took me to the Rhigos bookie, and I fainted inside.

The pair of them, Dad and Mam – the *Good Life* couple.

Mrs Marlene Morris

I am having the last word – which will not surprise Dai, Helen or Greg.

There are better qualified people to judge him as a rugby player. He must have been quite good to earn those caps, when they rarely played more than four times a year.

I know him as the man who leaves in the morning and comes back at night, and wouldn't harm a soul.

He can't be still for a minute. There is always something else to be done, someone else to see, animals to be checked, looked after, fed – not only ours, but Greg and Helen's too – lambs, chickens, horses and dogs. Then, every evening our elderly neighbour Alcwyn Davies is taken for an evening walk. All of this suggests that he is extremely organised.

Huh! Couldn't be further from the truth.

Dai Parker organises his social functions, and the kids and I do the rest.

His lateness for games was known throughout the village. People could set their clocks by him, because he'd leave everything to the last minute. He got caught out by heavy traffic once, and jumped out of the car, and ran all the way from Tonna to Neath, some five miles, to make kick-off.

He had a daily routine when he worked at the colliery, the welding factory and then with Walters Civil Engineering. He knew where he had to be and at what time. That was OK. Until very recently he was still getting up at the crack of dawn, six days a week, and returning well after dark from the Walters' stables in Cardiff.

He's not particularly good around the house. He'll make a cup of coffee, about once every three months. And in the evenings he'll ask whether I fancy a cuppa, but once he realises he'll have to make it himself, he'll go off the idea. Outside the front door is his world, where he has always been dedicated and hard working.

I didn't take that much note of his rugby career. My father watched him play for Glynneath, and sometimes I would enjoy a trip down to the Gnoll or Cardiff. I had a life and career of my own.

The one trip I did fancy was Paris in 1973. So I booked to go with the other wives, and was really looking forward to it. What happened? Tommy David was picked instead of Dai, and he couldn't travel as a reserve because of an ankle injury.

I'd booked and paid and went! I had a marvellous time, and Dai was at home probably attending to some animals.

I am not sure he could cope with retirement. I know he's seventy but he has to be busy.

He is totally devoted to us, the family. We are Number One. But the number of pets or strays we've had is nobody's business. There is a pet cemetery around the back. We've had a funeral service for every one of them. He's also passed on that love of animals to Helen and Greg, and the grandchildren, who have turned out the same.

And though he has played some of the toughest of opponents in the Welsh jersey – there is not a mean bone in his body. Dai Morris to us, the family, is a real softie – but only we are allowed to say that.

'Exposing the truth about the Regions and the
demise of rugby in the Welsh Valleys'

LYNN
Howells
Despite the knockbacks
Introductions by Graham Henry and Neil Jenkins

£9.95
Published November 2012

LYNN DAVIES

hard men
of WELSH
RUGBY

y Lolfa

£7.95

Shadow: The Dai Morris Story is just one of
a whole range of publications from Y Lolfa.
For a full list of books currently in print, send
now for your free copy of our new full-colour
catalogue. Or simply surf into our website

www.ylolfa.com

for secure on-line ordering.

TALYBONT CEREDIGION CYMRU SY24 5HE
e-mail ylolfa@ylolfa.com
website www.ylolfa.com
phone (01970) 832 304
fax 832 782